Component Training
For
Variable Surface Tracking

Ed Presnall
and
Christy Bergeon

PawMark Press

Acknowledgments

We are deeply grateful to John Barnard, Tracking Field Representative of the American Kennel Club, for his kind help in expanding our imagination concerning the abilities of our dogs and for the countless hours of discussion both during workshops and our continuing training process.

To our dogs, "JJ", "Ariel" and "Merlin" for being progressive and loving enough to put up with our training process and to our families for allowing us the time and freedom to pursue our dreams with our dogs. A special thank you goes out to Dale Nakashima and Barbara De Groodt for their kind assistance in the proofing and editing of this book.

No acknowledgment would be complete without mentioning "Ann", CT Sealair's Raggedy Ann, UD the first Champion Tracker, for making us believe that this quest was really possible.

Revised Edition 1998

PawMark Press

Box 6033 Katy, TX 77491

(c) Copyright 1998
Ed Presnall and Christy Bergeon
All rights Reserved

ISBN Number 0-9663092-0-0

Library of Congress Catalog Card Number: 98-96053

Cover Photo
Ch. Kay N Dee Hiddenbrook Rampage, CD, TD, VST
English Springer Spaniel

Photography
Ed Presnall, Christy Bergeon, Chris Presnall, Eric Hendrickson, Sue Ann Thompson
Illustrations
Ed Presnall

Table of Contents

Chapter 1

Introduction to Variable Surface Tracking

PHOTO BY CHRISTY BERGEON

According to the American Kennel Club Tracking Regulations, *"Tracking, by its nature, is a vigorous non-competitive outdoor sport. Tracking tests should demonstrate willingness and enjoyment by the dog in his work, and should always represent the best in sportsmanship and camaraderie by the people involved."*

This is, as most people involved in tracking have quickly learned, not only some "ivory tower" description of the sport, but is what the participants and their dogs live and breath. Your introduction to the sport may be just beginning or you might be an old timer with numerous T's and X's. Your introduction will hopefully be as enjoyable and rewarding as ours has been.

The tracking community itself is divided on the subject of Variable Surface Tracking. Some feel it is an unattainable goal due to the limited number of titles issued to date. Some feel that it is too difficult for the average dog to do and many believe that it can only be accomplished by dogs with a firm tracking foundation which includes the advanced TDX title.

Our belief is that any tracking dog can learn to work on non-vegetated surfaces and that it can, with proper motivation and training, be done at the same time you are training the dog for its first TD title. Each of the dogs we have worked with had only earned its TD title prior to starting on VST.

Our introduction started at a VST Workshop with an open mind and a desire to ask a sometimes never-ending stream of questions. We saw novice dogs, some with no tracking experience at all, execute short tracks on non-vegetated surfaces.

We thought that, if these novice dogs could *find it*, ours surely could and inquired of the few people who were training for the sport for more information. We learned that, unlike TD or TDX work, there was not a structured training method for this sport. Everyone seemed to be trying something different and sadly, very few were being successful.

We started evaluating potential VST sites, reviewing judge's maps from actual tests and matches and slowly, over a period of a few months, developed the method we call *Component Training*. We opened our minds and implemented a structured method of training, borrowing from the old and implementing new and creative ideas to enhance our dog's natural ability while expanding our learning experience.

The key point which we have learned about VST was, to say the least, unusual. Unlike other types of competition, *you can not **teach** a dog to track*. You can however, train to better understand your dog, condition it to the probable surroundings of a test, and learn how he/she indicates that they are *on-track* or lost.

Primarily VST is a tougher mental exercise than physical training problem. The dogs learn very quickly and pick up tracking on non-vegetated surfaces in a very brief time span. Their indications and perceived work ethics are usually not what we expect to see from a tracking dog. Our problem as trainers and handlers is to learn to read these new indications, which in most cases are radically different from what we are used to seeing in TD and TDX work. It requires a different type of training schedule, both in time, locations and tracklayers and it will require the handler to overcome some of the mental baggage we drag along concerning our fears over temperature, surfaces, contamination, people on the tracks, etc.

During your training for VST, you will develop a new understanding of how your dog works, what happens to scent under given conditions and most of all - a belief that VST is an achievable goal for you and your dog.

This guide by itself will not teach your dog to track on non-vegetated surfaces. It has allowed our dogs and those we train with to "fast track" the training process of variable surfaces. It will hopefully give you a better understanding of the sport of variable surface tracking, enhance your dog's natural ability to track and help to prepare you and your dog for test day.

Most of all, it will introduce you to another level of uncompetitive outdoor sport with your dog where you may train almost anywhere, at any time and in any weather conditions.

Hopefully, you, like thousands of other hard-core *trackers*, will continue to enjoy and support the sport.

Ed Presnall & Christy Bergeon
Spring 1998

Chapter 2

VST Basics

"Tracking is a team sport in the truest sense. In true team effort, a handler working as a team with his or her dog, exhibits a real understanding of the dog's motivation and commitment to the task at hand. The handler is able to read his or her dog and communicate with it to accomplish their goal. It is the responsibility of the Judges to differentiate between team cooperation and guiding by the handler and to determine when the handler is no longer a supporting member of that team and is attempting to guide the dog. In Variable Surface Tracking, team effort becomes even more critical due to the nature of the test. The objective of a Variable Surface Tracking Test is proving credibility in following a scent in an urban locale. The dog works for the sheer love of scenting."

We believe that VST, as John Barnard so politely put it in each of the VST workshops we have attended, is *"the future of tracking"*. The dogs that we have trained in VST have shown a remarkable capability to adjust to the changing surfaces and the perhaps added difficulty of the tracks. Is it really more difficult than X work? Physically, it is not, mentally, well that may be another matter.

VST has taught our dogs in part to follow the track whether it is on dirt, grass, asphalt, concrete or mulch. It has taught them that we can track at dawn or midnight, in a field, business park or inside a parking garage. And they know to be ready to track when the harness comes out, regardless of what time it is or what the weather may be.

An enjoyable benefit of VST work is the ability to always find a place to train, even if it is only a covered garage or shopping center parking lot. We do all of our training in highly contaminated areas such as schools, parking lots, malls, business parks and campus facilities. By working in these contaminated areas, we have in our belief, enhanced our dogs ability to discriminate scent and as a bonus made our training much easier for TDX work.

One of the first things we learned was to forget most of what we knew about our dogs and start over. We established a set schedule for our training periods and established in advance exactly what we were going to work on for that practice session.

Comparing VST to TD or TDX work is difficult, however we have established some of the following concepts.

In TD and TDX the test committee and judges attempt to keep the tracking area free of people and animals after the track is laid. In theory, many believe that they are tracking in a pristine field, uncluttered by other people or animal scent. But, in reality, scent stays in a given area for days and between the time the track was plotted and the next day when it was run, do we really know how many animals or people crossed the tracking area? In VST, there are no *clean* fields. You must assume that your dog, on test day, will be tracking across a parking lot which might have had an entire marching band there practicing only a few minutes before you walked up to the start flag.

In TDX, we know we will be faced with cross-tracks. Most established tracking methods emphasize that the dog must disregard or at least differentiate between animal or people cross tracks and stay focused on the tracklayer's scent. In VST, the cross-tracks are all over the tracking area. The dog must disregard not only two sets of cross-tracks, but perhaps hundreds. You must introduce your dog to pedestrians along the track, automobiles, parked cars, doors and entrance ways to buildings and areas contaminated by other dogs. In VST, *expect the unexpected* and train for it.

In TDX we know we will be faced with obstacles. To prepare ourselves for test day, we train our TDX dogs on ditches, fences, road crossings, hills and other various obstacles which they might encounter along their track. In VST we simply train for a different type of non-physical obstacle. Obstacles which can push or gather scent or appear to have different properties on different days due to changing wind or weather conditions.

VST has given us the opportunity to train when we wanted to. We don't have to get up at the crack of dawn to lay tracks before the fields heat up to the point we cannot work in them. We can track in shorts and a t-shirt and just tennis shoes and let me tell you when the temperatures are in the 90's and the humidity is almost 100%, that is one of the many rewarding features of VST!

During our introduction to VST, we were told to train in an *urban* setting, around buildings. Each of the workshops we attended were in campus locations with buildings. The tests were designed to be held in business parks and campus locations. That to us meant around buildings whether it was written in the regulation or not. We train for buildings, and cars, and people, and standing water in parking lots and a hundred other possibilities that we might be confronted with on test day.

We have never looked at VST as a solution to the lack of space to hold TD or TDX tests. We looked at it as an opportunity to expand our dogs abilities, learn more about how scent really travels, and most of all to test out training techniques and theory on our dogs with an achievable goal of the title. Most of all we look at VST as fun.

It comes down to a very basic belief - if you believe in the concept of VST, then work within the current guidelines. Plot the tracks in suitable locations to the best of your ability. Accept advice from others who offer it, or give advice to those who might request it, you can be successful in your quest for a *Variable Surface Tracker* title.

Ed Presnall with *Merlin* and Christy Bergeon with *Ariel*
Both Earn VST Titles in Wheaton, IL. October 5, 1997
Glenbard All Breed Obedience Club
Judges Wally O'Brien and Darlene Ceretto

Chapter 3

What is VST?

PHOTO BY ED PRESNALL

Commitment

Variable Surface Tracking, like any other form of tracking requires a commitment by you to spend the time required to work with your dog. In our training program, we have been successful in motivating our dogs and progressing through the training process in a relatively short period of time. However, each dog is different and each handler must make the commitment to work and train for a sufficient period of time to master most of the individual components of VST. This can happen, as in our case, in a period as short as seven months or may require that you spend several years working with your dog.

Purpose

The Variable Surface Tracking Test is a test of credibility, verifying the dog's ability to recognize and follow human scent while adapting to changing scenting conditions. The test is to be as practical as possible while demonstrating the dog's willingness and ability to follow a specific scent which is given to the dog at the start of the test. The training and conditioning of the dog must be designed to develop the inner drive, motivation and determination necessary for the dog to work with intensity and perseverance.

Intent

"All tracks shall be laid utilizing buildings and the diverse scenting conditions created by being in close proximity to such buildings. Tracks shall also utilize any and/all other structures such as fences, breezeways, ramps, stairs, bridges, shelters, roofed parking garages, through courtyards and buildings with two or more openings and/or open buildings. The intent of Variable Surface Tracking stresses that dogs shall be able to handle the diffusion of scent created by these structures. Tracks shall be as equal in complexity as possible in this regard. Tracks may not enter a building with closed doors and sides."

As we work in VST and as VST grows up as a sport, we each continue to learn. Perhaps in some cases we can learn more from our mistakes or problems we encounter along the track than from our successes. Working as a training team, we must continue to challenge each other and the dogs with new training methods, motivational ideas and component configurations.

When VST started, only a few years ago, it was a concept and a fairly radical change from traditional TD and TDX tracking. Only a handful of people in the tracking community had been attempting to track while on non-vegetated surfaces. No one had ever laid a track in a test. The judges and track layers were untested, and many exhibitors felt that if their dog had a TDX title, this alone qualified them to compete in VST.

It was a learning experience and an eye opener for all of us. The first VST tracks in our area were in a State Park normally used for TD's and occasional X tracks. Since it was a combined TD/VST test the Judges utilized grass, gravel, dirt, a graveyard, blacktop roads and large asphalt parking lots. At the time, due to our learning about VST, such tracks were considered acceptable, however, there were no dogs entered with much if any VST experience. Did it make them bad tracks? Not necessarily, but at it was a location which was available to the Club and both the judges and exhibitors were there for a learning experience.

Was it the judges intent to lay long "T-tracks" with minimal variable surfaces? No. The tracks utilize approximately 40% non-vegetated areas. The majority of this is dirt, gravel and pea-gravel sidewalks. Such surfaces, we have now learned hold scent. A turn on a sidewalk, one near the woods, one paralleling a roadway and another down a two lane blacktop road were the major challenges for the dog.

By today's standards, they were not difficult tracks. The tracks had a tendency to lead the dogs away from the track with the amount of woods, hedges, rock walls, fences, etc. Most dogs today, continue to fail on the vegetated portion of the tracks.

The community was divided. Comments about VST came from everywhere, and everyone it seemed, had an opinion. Some said that VST was too hard for the dogs to be successful. Another concern was whether the dogs could track on asphalt or concrete surfaces that could become too hot.

One real problem, both then and today, was that most people did not understand scent or how to train dogs to work in highly contaminated areas. Judges were approved, only because they attended an introductory workshop and yet had no hands on experience in working dogs on non-vegetated surfaces. Some tests were held at locations that were typically used for TD and TDX tracks and everyone learned.

What resulted the first few years was frustrating to the tracking community and those few handlers who actually believed that VST was possible. They worked and trained only to be faced at a test, in some cases, with unsuitable locations or poorly thought out and planned tracks. This was not an attempt by the judges to plot bad tracks or to fail dogs, it was only an indication of the additional training which is required to understand scent conditions, the effect of buildings and wind on portions of the tracks.

Now several years later, VST is a reality which has been and continues to be refined by both the judges and exhibitors. It is the intent for a VST test to be held in areas such as business parks and campus locations and *around* buildings. Training your dog in these locations is imperative.

Expect the unexpected

Train for and expect

- ☐ For your track to start in a highly contaminated area such as next to the exhibitor and headquarters parking area.

- ☐ For your track, to have a short vegetated leg and then transition to non-vegetated surfaces.

- ☐ For halting your dog to allow traffic to pass or pedestrians to talk to or pet your dog.

- ☐ For crossing roads and parking lots with moving traffic.

- ☐ For your track to run down sidewalks or roadways while dodging pedestrians or moving traffic.

- ☐ For your track to parallel or go down roadways.

- ☐ For your track to run up to building entrances, stairways, wheelchair ramps or other such public areas around buildings.

- ☐ For your dog to be approached by strangers wanting to pet him, ask directions or distract you and your dog with questions about what you are doing.

- ☐ For your track to run through sprinklers, standing water at curbs, or water running across a parking lot or street.

- ☐ For your track to turn at chain link fences, buildings or sidewalks.

- ☐ For your track to cross or turn on mulch, grass, gravel or stone islands in or near parking lots.

- ☐ For your track to run between parked cars and moving traffic.

- ☐ For your track to run through a "tunnel" of buildings and/or fencing.

PHOTO BY ED PRESNALL

Chapter 4

VST Requirements

Variable Surface Tracking Test Requirements

The following are the restrictions and minimum requirements for a Variable Surface Track:

☐ The track shall be at least 600 yards and not more than 800 yards in length.

☐ The track shall have a minimum of three (3) different surfaces, which shall include vegetation and two areas devoid of vegetation, such as concrete, asphalt, gravel, sand, hard pan or mulch. The areas devoid of vegetation shall comprise at least one-third (1/3) to one-half (1/2) of the total length of the track.

All tracks shall be laid utilizing buildings and the diverse scenting conditions created by being in close proximity to such buildings. Tracks shall also utilize any and/all other structures such as fences, breezeways, ramps, stairs, bridges, shelters, roofed parking garages, through court-yards and buildings with two or more openings and/or open buildings. The intent of Variable Surface Tracking stresses that dogs shall be able to handle the diffusion of scent created by these structures. Tracks shall be as equal in complexity as possible in this regard. Tracks may not enter a building with closed doors and sides.

☐ No part of the track shall be within fifty (50) yards of any other track. No part of the track may be within thirty (30) yards of any other part of the same track.

☐ The track shall be plotted using different surfaces and scenting conditions as afforded by the terrain. There shall be no physical obstacles or obstructions such as are used on a TDX track. The level of physical difficulty should be such that it will permit all AKC breeds and handlers of any age to participate. Ordinary stair steps are not considered to be an obstacle, but a wall or fence which must be climbed over or scaled is an obstruction that must be avoided.

☐ The scent on the track shall be not less than three (3) hours nor more than five (5) hours old.

☐ To further establish credibility, articles used in Variable Surface Tracking represent items made of substances used in everyday life that an average child or adult might carry and drop.

After the starting article of leather or fabric, Judges should make every effort to place the remaining articles in varying random order on all tracks. Judges should not use standardized articles so handlers are not looking for only certain articles or a definite sequence of articles. Article drop 2 or 3 should be on a non-vegetated surface. This does not preclude the track from ending on a non-vegetated surface and the final article also being on a non-vegetated surface.

The last article should be temporarily marked with the number 4, such as with a small post it note cut down in size, but NOT WITH any permanent markers or grease type pencils. Articles should not have any rough edges or any protruding parts that might cause injury to the dog.

☐ The handler may pick up the article at the starting flag and use it, as well as subsequent articles, to give scent to the dog while on the track.

☐ Snow, frost, dew on the fields, plowed ground, or on any other vegetated or non-vegetated surface such as in a VST test, creates the possibility that the path of the tracklayer may be evident to the dog and handler. Judges must consider whether awarding a title to a dog under these circumstances would render a disservice to all previous title holders who have truly earned their titles. If the Judges decide to proceed on any field or variable surface tracking area where the track is visible, they must be alert to any attempt by a handler to lead his dog. Any indication of guidance by the handler shall cause the dog to fail. It is especially critical in VST that there are three (3) different surfaces available and that these surfaces are not obscured by a covering such as snow, otherwise the intent of VST will not be met.

☐ Turns shall be on various surfaces as dictated by the terrain. There shall be at least four (4) and not more than eight (8) turns on a track. Both right and left turns shall be used. At least three (3) of the turns shall be right angle (90 degree) turns and there should be more than three (3) such turns. Tracks may be laid along the sides of buildings and fences, through buildings with two or more openings or open sided, such as breezeways, shelters or roofed parking garages, but may not enter a building with closed doors and sides. At least one (1) 90 degree turn shall be in an area devoid of vegetation and plotted to allow at least thirty (30) yards before crossing or returning to a vegetated surface. Acute angle turns are to be avoided.

☐ Should an animal, pedestrian or vehicular traffic appear or move across the track, the dog and handler will continue to work the track, as incidents such as these are considered a normal occurrence for this test.

Established 2-98

General Requirements:

☐   Plotting a spare track is not required.

☐   Both Judges must walk every track and plot all tracks together.

☐   A previously used track may not be run either forward or backward within three (3) days of use.

☐   The same Tracklayer may not be used on contiguous tracks.

☐   In the case of Variable Surface Tracking, for the safety of the dog and handler, Judges must be cognizant of surface temperatures in hot weather, especially on asphalt and concrete. Tracks shall not be run on surfaces where the Judges and/or tracking committee have knowledge of recent treatment with chemicals that might cause an injury to the dog and handler. If conditions are such as to be unsafe for the dog and handler, the test shall be delayed, postponed or canceled.

☐   In Variable Surface Tracking, Judges, exhibitors, spectators and test giving clubs should be aware that these areas may be heavily used by the general public and accordingly, must make every effort to cooperate with these public areas and the people who use them in order to ensure that these variable surface tracking sites will continue to be available for future tests. Clubs and exhibitors alike must try to confine "exercise areas" for dogs to a small designated area and be sure that those areas are cleaned up before the test is over and the area is left in the same condition as it was at the start of the test, not only to promote responsible dog ownership but to promote good relations with the general public.

☐   In Variable Surface Tracking, although there are no physical obstacles as found in TDX, handlers must train for all types of conditions and surfaces that might be commonly found in a variable surface tracking area, such as soft and hard dirt, blacktop, concrete, paving materials, sand, gravel, wood chips or metal stairs and to train for the diverse scenting conditions that exist in variable surface tracking.

☐   Only contamination of a track by a hazardous material, or a large portion of a track being rendered unusable, will warrant another track being laid. People, animals, or vehicles crossing a track shall not invalidate that track.

☐   A Variable Surface Tracking site totally or partially covered in snow would not meet the criteria of three (3) different surfaces including vegetated and non-vegetated surfaces and snow covered portions of a Variable Surface Tracking site may seriously affect the proper utilization of the site as a whole.

Established 2-98

TRACKING COMPARISON CHART

	TD	TDX	VST
ELIGIBILITY	6 Months of age with certification	TD Title	TD Title with 6 months between title and VST closing date
START	Direction of track indicated by start flag and one flag 30 yards out. Test starts when dog leaves the 1st flag.	Only start flag in arc of 180°, no direction given. Test starts when dog leaves the start flag.	Only start flag in arc of 180°, if possible on vegetated surface proceeding for at least 15 yards before change of surface. No direction given. Test starts when dog leaves the start flag.
LENGTH	440 - 500 yards	800 - 1000 yards	600 - 800 yards
LEG LENGTH	Minimum of 50 yards	Minimum of 50 yards	Minimum of 30 yards
SCENT	That of a stranger	That of a stranger	That of a stranger
AGE	1/2 hour - 2 hours	3 hours - 5 hours	3 hours - 5 hours
TURNS	Both right and left must be used; There shall be 3-5 turns with at least 2 right angle turns. Acute turns prohibited.	Both right and left must be used; There shall be 5-7 turns with at least 3 right angle turns. Acute turns discouraged.	Both right and left must be used; There shall be 4-8 turns with at least 3 right angle turns. Acute turns discouraged. At least 1 right angle turn shall be on non-vegetated area for a distance of at least 30 yards before a change in surface.
RESTART	One permitted, with judges' permission if dog has not passed 2nd start flag.	None allowed	None allowed
CROSSTRACKS	None	2 Cross tracklayers about 4 feet apart; at 2 widely separated points on track. None on first leg.	No formal cross tracks plotted. Naturally occurring cross scent of people, animals, vehicles, etc. accepted as a natural part of the test.
DISTANCE BETWEEN TRACKS	75 yards	75 yards	50 yards
TEST MAX ENTRY	12	6	8

	TD	TDX	VST
OBSTACLES	None	At least 2, but none on the 1st leg.	None such as used on TDX tracks. But ordinary stairs, open buildings, shelters, garages, are acceptable; no closed buildings.
ARTICLES	One, inconspicuous glove or waller at the end.	Four, personal, dissimilar, about the size of glove or wallet placed along the track, at least 30 yards from a turn, cross track or obstacle.	Four dissimilar, everyday items; 2"x5" to 5"x5", weighing no more than 8 oz.; fabric, leather, rigid or semi-rigid plastic and metal. Fabric or leather **must** be the starting article. The last article must be marked with a #4. Articles to be placed along the track at Judges' discretion. At least 1 article is to be placed on non-vegetated surface, all articles to be placed at least 10 yards from a turn.
WORKING LEASH LENGTH	20 feet from dog, leash marked	20 feet from dog, leash marked	10 feet from dog, leash **not** marked
TERRAIN	Typical TD field	Typical TDX field	At least 3 different surfaces, including both vegetated and non-vegetated areas. Non-vegetated areas will comprise at least 1/3 to 1/2 of the track length.
SPARE TRACK	Recommended	Recommended	Not Necessary

SPECIAL NOTES:

A safety person may be appointed to watch for moving vehicles and other potential hazards in an urban area for the protection of dog and handler.

Provided the dog is working continuously and intently along the track and an article cannot be located by the Judges and/or tracklayer, the dog will be given credit for the article without actively indicating the area.

Substitution factor of 2 TDs = 1 TDX or 1 VST; 1 TDX = 1 VST. Combinations may be used up to a maximum equal to 12 TDs or 6 TDXs or VSTs in one day.

A dog earning all 3 tracking titles of TD, TDX and VST will be considered a Champion Tracker (CT).

PHOTO BY ERIC HENDRICKSON

Chapter 5

Scent and VST

PHOTO BY ED PRESNALL

Scent: What is the dog following?

Many people have tried to define what scent is. Webster defines it as *"an emanation from a substance that effects the sense of smell"* or *"an odor left by an animal or person by which it is tracked in hunting"*.

As a person walks through a field, his scent is embedded into the grass, dirt and brush. The scent is a combination of body scent, individual chemical make-up of the person, the fabric and texture of their clothes and footwear, soap, perfume, deodorant, hair spray, smoke odor and their body weight. The basis of the individuality of each person's scent is thought by scientists to come from a natural skin lubricant called *sebum*.

Scent and its lasting effect is affected by weather conditions; dry, wet, cold, warm, snow, rain, fog, mist, sun, wind, age of the track, altitude and the type of ground cover.

On a hot, dry day in a dusty field, the scent will be harder for the dog to follow. If the wind picks up, it gets more difficult. While on a damp, cool morning, with little wind, the dog will follow the track as if it were on rails. For beginner track layers trying to define scent and its use in tracking involves lots of complications, too many variables and a great deal of frustration. Go back to the "KISS" method. The longer the grass, the stronger the scent. The lower the wind, the stronger the ground scent. Most importantly, trust your dog. A dog can easily determine over 10,000 different scents, you can't.

After years of research by the government, scientists, enthusiasts and other trackers, we have concluded as William R. Koehler so eloquently put it *"We humans cannot track by scent and know little of scent's mysteries, so obviously there is no positive way we can make a dog use his ability to track."*

Types of Scent

□ Ground Scent

Ground scent is a trail of molecular level smells left on the ground, on the grass and brush which is touched or stepped on by a persons walking over the terrain.

□ Airborne Scent

Airborne scent is the molecular level smell distributed by wind currents either upwind or downwind of the original ground scent.

□ What Seems To Affect Scent

❖ **Weather:**
   □ Temperature
   □ Humidity
   □ Rain
   □ Fog
   □ Mist
   □ Standing Moisture
   □ Sunlight
   □ Wind

❖ **Track Age:**
   □Contrary to what many people seem to think, we feel that in VST the longer the track has aged, the easier it is for the dog to follow it. Fresh tracks, under 1 hour in age, sometimes seem to be *too hot* for the dog to stay exactly on the track. Once the scent cone has dispersed and the majority of the scent which remains is in the footsteps, typically 3 to 5 hours, the dog has an easier time of staying on the track and negotiating non-vegetated turns.

❖ **Ground Cover or Surface Changes:**
   □ Changes in the height of grasses
   □ Curbs, sidewalks
   □ Painted stripes in parking lots
   □ Closeness to building or structures
   □ Hedges, fences and walls

❖ **Altitude and Humidity:**
   □Typically, the higher the elevation, the faster the scent tends to age. In low humidity areas you will find your dog working harder and appearing to have less scent to follow. In higher humidity areas, the tracks will not age as fast and the scent will be held closer to the actual footsteps of the tracklayer.

Most dogs can determine the difference between the two scent trails and most will alternate their tracking by lifting their noses from the "footsteps" to sniff the wind as they work a track. As changes in terrain or conditions occur during the track, the dog may favor one of these trails over another. Your basic objective in training will be to try to keep your dog's nose "glued" to the ground.

The easiest method of accomplishing this is to utilize short training tracks with a reasonable amount of ground cover. To make it easier for your dog, plot the track through a field of grass, rather than across a parking lot. As your dog becomes aware of what VST tracking is all about, and you become more accomplished in "reading" your dog, you will vary your tracking site to include short grass, long grass, mulch, dirt, gravel, asphalt and concrete to enhance your dogs ability to work on various surfaces.

To help you grasp the concept of scent, attempt to think about your track in the following manner. Pretend that the scent you are leaving as you lay a track is a heavy fog. As you walk through the field, this fog clings to the ground, grass and any hedge or building you might walk by.

Now consider that if a wind is blowing, the fog will drift along the ground in the direction the wind is blowing. The fog will also collect or become saturated in low spots, along fences or hedges, in and next to ditches or culverts or simply next to changes in the height of grasses.

A change in height as small as the paint on a stripe in a parking lot or the depression made by an edger next to a sidewalk is enough to hold the scent.

Think about this as you lay the track and again while you are watching your dog search for the track. It will give you a better appreciation for the working ability of your dog's nose.

Remember, the dog has the advantage with its ability to differentiate between approximately 500,000 different scents using its 100 million or so olfactory cells, versus our ability to only differentiate between several thousand scents using our 5 million olfactory cells.

PHOTO BY ED PRESNALL

Chapter 6

Basic Rules of Tracking

Basic Rules of VST Tracking

- [ ] You can not teach your dog to track! Your dog like all others has the natural ability to track. In tracking, you will enforce your dog's desire to track if and only if it pleases him to do something for you or for food, praise or other motivation. Do not get upset or frustrated at your dog, remember, of everyone in the field, he is the only one who can track. Make it easy and make it fun.

- [ ] No scolding or chastisement whatever are permitted when in the tracking area.

- [ ] Down, sit or stand your dog at the start flag for a period of time long enough for him to gather in the required scent.

- [ ] Never leave the start flag without the start article.

- [ ] The tracking harness does not go on the dog at any other time except when the handler and dog are about to commence a track. It is removed at the end of the track <u>before</u> leaving the tracking area. Our point is to condition the dog to prepare to track when the harness comes out and continue to track until we remove the harness.

- [ ] The tracklayer *must* draw a map for all tracks and must follow the handler while the dog completes the track or training exercise.

- [ ] All dogs must be watered immediately following a track -- before the handler and tracklayer -- before discussions -- before anything. Depending on your part of the country, it is advisable to always cary water with you on the track.

☐   Know exactly what you are trying to accomplish before you arrive at the training site.

☐   Plan the layout of your track before you start. Drive around the site, determine the legs, turns and possible article placement before you start.

☐   No dogs are to be released from their leads while on the tracking area. The tracking area is for *tracking work* and is not to be confused with play, obedience, conformation or retrieving.

☐   Investigate every time your dog stops for an article. If in doubt, go look.

☐   No leads longer than 20 feet. The closer you work to your dog, the more confidence you will communicate to him.

PHOTO BY CHRISTY BERGEON

Chapter 7

Tracking Terminology

Tracking Terminology

Acute Turn A turn of less than 90 degrees.

Age / Aging The amount of time elapsed from the track layer starting to lay the track until the dog starts to follow the track.

Article Four common, everyday items which can be easily carried by the tracklayer and safely picked up by the dog. Articles are placed at the start and end of the track with two dispersed on the track itself. Each article shall not be smaller than 2" x 5" nor larger than 5" x 5" and weigh no more than 8 ounces. In VST, one article is leather, one plastic (rigid or semi-rigid), one metal and one fabric article. The first article is always fabric or leather and the last article will be marked with the number "4."

Backtrack Retracing steps over a portion of the track that has already been completed. Also known as "double laying" or triple laying" a track.

Blind Track A track laid by another person and totally unknown to the handler. No flags or turn markers are used. An exact map is required to plot this kind of track.

Body English *by the dog*: movements made by the dog that can be interpreted by the handler. Examples are ear movement, tail wagging, lifting of head other body movements.

by the handler: voluntary or involuntary movements that influence the dog's action. Also known as guiding the dog.

Guiding
Examples include: turning your body toward a turn, pulling or moving the lead to force the dog to change direction, restraining or refusing to follow your dog.

Cast
Stray or wander off-track by more than 3 feet on either side or to circle at turns.

Conditioning
Builds up the dog's, or the handler's physical ability and endurance to walk through the fields and follow the track.

Coursing
Sweeping back-and-forth across the track in wide arcs.

Cover Changes
Changes in track surface. The cover may go from short grass to bare ground, to asphalt, to mulch, to concrete, to dirt, etc.

Crosswind
Blowing in any direction not parallel to the track.

Downwind
Blowing from the dog and handlers back. Also defined as "With the Wind".

Fouled Track
A track which has been compromised by an unplanned scent. Although highly unusual in VST, a chemical spill, treatment of a track area by pesticides or a hazard to the dog or handler could cause a track to be declared fouled.

Fringe
The immediate area, approximately 3 feet in width, on either side of the primary track.

Inductive Training
Shaping behavior with positive reinforcement such as food and praise.

Leg
Segment of a track between the start and the first turn or between subsequent turns.

Non-restrictive Harness
Light-weight, durable and adjustable leather, nylon webbing or canvas harness that does not restrict the dog's shoulder movement.

Obstacle
Unlike TDX work, there are no physical obstacles or obstructions on a VST track. VST obstacles are primarily scent discrimination problems caused by structures, buildings, walls, fences, etc.

Obtuse Turn   Oblique or open turn of more than 90 degrees.

Plot   To lay out a track and/or make a map. Also defined as "chart".

Primary Track   The track the dog is to follow.

Scuffing   Dragging of tracklayer's feet to leave a very concentrated scent.

Steptracking   Scenting from one footprint to another. Beneficial in finding articles, sorting out primary tracks from cross-tracks, and working older and/or longer tracks.

Upwind   Blowing towards the dog's face. Also defined as "Into the Wind".

PHOTO BY ED PRESNALL

Chapter 8

Equipment

Equipment

☐ **Harness -** Non-restrictive harness. Leather or woven nylon.

☐ **Lead -** Woven nylon or cotton lead. Depending on your dogs breed and pulling ability, the lead may be 3/8, 1/2, 3/4 or 1 inch in width. You will need both a 6 foot and a 20 foot lead. The regulations state that you can work as close as ten feet from your dog. Being close to the dog keeps him closer to the track while enhancing your ability to watch the dog's subtle actions and offers additional confidence and motivation to your dog while it is working.

☐ **Waist Bag -** An article bag or bird bag to carry articles, water and other supplies while you are training or exhibiting in a test. In training situations, you will find that a larger or multiple pocket bag will be required. On a normal training session, we may carry 10 or more articles while in some of these exercises we utilize as many as 30 articles.

☐ **Article Bag/Box -** A soft sided overnight bag, small duffle or suitable box will be required to maintain your selection of articles. Our bags typically contain from 50 to 80 articles in various sizes and colors in cloth, leather, metal and plastic.

☐ **Article**s - Common, everyday items to leave on the track for the dog to find. In VST, articles are so varied, we've added an entire chapter to discuss them.

☐ **Starting flags -** Any size or color. We prefer to use short, colored surveyor flags as they tend to blend into the surroundings along with telephone, gas and electric company flags left by repair crews. Since they blend in, there is less chance of a passerby walking up to the start flag and disturbing the start area or removing the start article.

- ☐ **Food or motivational instruments** - Food can range from puppy biscuits, to liver, Rollover, Oinker Roll, kibble, etc. A motivational instrument is your dogs favorite toy, ball or plaything. We are not going to get involved in the food *vs.* no food methods of training. We have worked with dogs that required food to motivate them to track on non-vegetated surfaces and dogs which were happy to track for their ball, favorite toy or simply for praise.

- ☐ **Water** - Easily carried in "sports" bottles for refreshing your dog on the track. Even when tracking on non-vegetated areas in low elevations and cool weather your dog may need to be refreshed along the track. If your training area is at higher elevations or lower humidity, or you are training in higher temperatures you may need to refresh your dog more frequently. Always carry a larger water supply and bowl for your dog after you finish the track. In extremely hot weather, you may need to soak or wet down your dog prior to and after running the track to reduce the body temperature.

- ☐ **Shoes/footgear** - The type of shoes or boots worn is not important in tracking. Dogs have consistently and successfully tracked bare feet, socks, tennis shoes, hiking boots and rubber boots. Make sure the shoes you select to wear are comfortable and suited to your climate and weather patterns. Carry an extra pair or rain boots just in case of inclement weather.

- ☐ **First aid kit** - As with any form of tracking a first aid kit is an essential item to carry in your car. Basic items include insect spray, meat tenderizer for insect bites, gauze or tourniquet material in case of snake bite, alcohol, gauze pads for cuts and scrapes on you or your dog, ophthalmic ointment and eye wash for irritated eyes.

- ☐ **Wrist watch** - In training and in recording your progress through the various components, you will be recording the ageing of your tracks.

- ☐ **Tracking log** - A must. Recording each training track will allow you to work through this workbook and follow the progress of your dog. Samples of the logs we use are included in the back of the workbook for your convenience.

- ☐ **AKC Tracking Regulations** - Read the rules and know the rules. Each of the components outlined in this book are based on actual VST tracks which were laid in VST Tracking Tests. When you understand the rules, you will lay better tracks, enabling you and your dog to approach the start of the track in a test without apprehension.

PHOTO BY CHRISTY BERGEON

Chapter 9

Articles

PHOTO BY CHRISTY BERGEON

Articles

The AKC Tracking Regulations in Section 5. Articles for Variable Surface Tracking Test, states that *"... VST articles shall consist of four (4) dissimilar, common, everyday items which can be easily carried by the Tracklayer and safely picked up by the dog. Each article shall not be smaller than 2" x 5" nor larger than 5" x 5" and weigh no more than 8 ounces.*

There shall be one leather, one plastic (rigid or semi-rigid), one metal and one fabric article which shall be handled by the Tracklayer, and are to be dropped on the track by the Tracklayer at the points indicated on the Judges' charts."

That description of articles leaves it wide open for the tracklayers and judges to select articles to use for both training and actual tests. We work with a very large selection of articles to keep the dogs from becoming comfortable with a static set and due to the inherent loss of articles while working in populated areas.

"To further establish credibility, articles used in Variable Surface Tracking represent items made of substances used in everyday life that an average child or adult might carry and drop. After the starting article of leather or fabric, Judges should make every effort to place the remaining articles in varying random order on all tracks. Judges should not use standardized articles so handlers are not looking for only certain articles or a definite sequence of articles."

"Article drop 2 or 3 should be on a non-vegetated surface. This does not preclude the track from ending on a non-vegetated surface and the final article also being on a non-vegetated surface. The last article should be temporarily marked with the number 4, such as with a small post it note cut down in size, but NOT WITH any permanent markers or grease type pencils. Articles should not have any rough edges or any protruding parts that might cause injury to the dog."

As a basis for what type of articles you should use, we feel that if you can carry it, the dog can pick it up and it is safe, use it. We tend to haunt the secondhand shops, toy stores, our kids rooms, hardware stores and always watch for something new to be used at a test. We do not use crushed cans of any type due to the possibility of the dog being cut or hurt.

Article Placement

"When determining the placement of articles on the track, Judges should keep in mind the possibility that under certain wind conditions and circumstances, if an article is placed on a minimum length leg (30 yards) connecting two parallel legs, the dog might easily bypass that minimum leg and article, thereby failing. Judges are discouraged from placing articles in such fashion as to fail dogs. Judges should also use caution in placing articles in or near buildings and structures when there is a strong possibility that the dog might cut off that portion of the leg that the article is on."

It is imperative when working on components or full-length tracks that you carefully consider your article placement. As the above regulations show, it is possible for the dog to miss an article solely based on its placement.

Missing Articles

In VST, it is probable that at some point in your training or at a test an article will be missing. In a test, if the missing article is the start article, the judges will authorize a replacement article. If the missing article is numbers 2, 3 or 4, the regulations provide the following solution.

If, in the Judges' opinion, the dog actively searched the area where an article was dropped but did not find the article, and the Judges cannot find the article, the dog shall be given credit for finding the article.

Plan a part of your training program to include restarting your dog at a *lost* article. As you lay components or tracks, stop at a location where you have planned to place an article. Drop the article and then pick it up and continue on. or have another person cross your track and retrieve the article. Watch to see if your dog indicates that there *was* an article at that location. Praise him and continue on with your track.

PHOTO BY ED PRESNALL

The following is a partial listing of some of the articles used in our training program as well as those we have seen or found in tests.

Plastic Articles

birth control pill case	can lid (coffee, etc.)	car door parts
car tail light lens	Legos ™	kids meal toys
jar lid	CD-Rom	credit/key access card
eye glass case	toy bird wing	PCV ™ sheets (4x4")
wallet	comb	diskette
brush	picture frames	Zip ™ disk case
comb case	hair brush	PCV ™ pipe (various sizes)
light switch cover	plastic belt	diskette case
medicine bottle	kids toys (cars/trucks.etc.)	sign reflector
change purse	small boxes	key fob

Metal Articles

belt buckle (brass)	belt buckle (chrome)	belt buckle (steel)
belt buckle (tin)	boxes	car door handle
can / jar lids	car emblems	door hinge (brass)
door hinge (steel)	diesel truck emblem	electrical box
electrical box cover	Erector Set ™ pieces	large brass connector
keys & keychains	kids toys (cars, trucks, etc.)	light switch (aluminum)
light switch (brass)	light switch (chrome)	light switch (tin)
light switch (zinc)	pipe (aluminum)	pipe (brass)
pipe (chrome)	pipe (galvanized)	pipe (steel)
spring (brass)	spring (steel)	checkbook cover

Cloth Articles

gloves	ties	hats
washcloth	clothing parts	panties
bras	socks	checkbook cover
bandana	scarf	wrist-band

Leather Articles

gloves	coin purse	hat brim
wallet	keychain	strips of leather
drink coaster	clothing	belts
eye glass case	purse	checkbook cover

Chapter 10

Basic Map Making

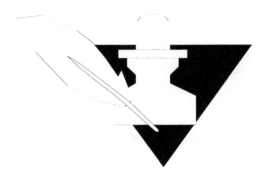

Basic Map Making

Learning how to accurately plot or chart a map is a *must skill* for all trackers and track layers. The written record of your track is mandatory when you are laying the track as well as when you are following your dog. In VST, whether working on components or a complete training track, this record will assist you in evaluating your dog. It will also allow you to have an accurate record of exactly where the track is ... and when the dog is off track or is having problems with a specific component.

In VST, it is almost impossible to remember all of the landmarks that designate your track. Curbs, lines in parking lots, manhole covers or light poles all tend to look alike. With a map of your component or track, you can easily refer to that component and know that the turn is at the seventh stripe in the parking lot and is lined up with the entrance to the building.

Attempting to work VST tracks without accurate maps may do more harm than good. Continually calling the dog off-track or following the dog off-track are considered by some as the worst and most common training errors.

The maps you will make should be detailed enough for you to return to the same training area on another day and re-lay an identical track. The best thing that I can tell you about map making is ... stop, look and then write. If you get in a hurry, your map will reflect it in a lack of detail.

The fundamentals of map making are quite easy. They include:

        ☐   Map Making Equipment
        ☐   Determining The Length Of Your Stride
        ☐   Walking A Straight Line
        ☐   Locating 2 Objects In Your Path
        ☐   Start Flag and Articles

    ☐   Landmarks

    ☐   Ground Markers

    ☐   Compass Headings

    ☐   Distance

    ☐   Time

    ☐   Weather Conditions

    ☐   Ground Conditions

☐ Map Making Equipment

You will need a clipboard, paper and a pencil and a couple of large rubber bands. Many people like to tie the pencil or pen onto the clipboard with a string. This is easier than dropping the pencil and searching for it while you are being pressured to "lay a track." For rain or wet weather, a supply of clear mylar or waterproof paper is required.

A sample map making form has been included in this chapter. It is a version of the formal American Kennel Club judges form. We have slightly modified the form to better meet our needs, and to help us to remember to write all of the information down.

Many track layers use a simple notebook or even blank paper to plot their maps. This is a personal matter and every track layer I have met has their own idea about what is best for them.

☐ Determining The Length Of Your Stride

In order for you to prepare and plot accurate tracks and maps, you must determine the length of your stride and how to convert that length into actual yardage. All declaration of length in tracking, whether verbally, written on maps or in an actual test, should be stated in yards.

To determine the length of your stride, start by measuring a 300 foot line across your typical tracking area, down a city street or through a vacant lot. Mark the start and finish. In our training area, we use a can of spray paint to make a small mark on a curb at the start and another small mark at the end. In this manner, the markings remain for several months allowing us to reuse the stride area over and over.

Walk this distance using your normal tracking stride and count how many paces it is. Write the number of paces down and then turn around and walk back, again counting the paces. Write this number down.

Average the two numbers by adding them together and dividing the sum by 2. This is the number of paces that you need to walk to cover 100 yards on a track.

The following table will help you determine the length of your tracking stride.

Distance - 100 Yards

Number of Paces 1 : _____   Number of Paces 2 : _____

(1) _____ + (2) _____ = _____ /2 = _____ = paces/100 yards

Now divide the Number of Strides per 100 Yards to complete the following chart.

Length of Your Stride *vs.* Yards

# of Yards	Steps	# of Yards	Steps
10	_____	75	_____
20	_____	100	_____
30	_____	125	_____
40	_____	150	_____
50	_____	200	_____

Copy this chart and tape it to your clipboard.

☐   **Walking A Straight Line**

In order for you to learn to track, you must first learn how to walk in a straight line. It may sound funny, but most people simply cannot walk in a straight line. Try the following to demonstrate this action.

Plant a tracking flag in the ground next to your left foot. Walk approximately 100 yards away, plant a second flag next to your left foot and turn around. Looking at the first flag, walk straight to it, planting a flag next to your left foot every 10 yards. Look only forward, towards the first flag, not back were you came from. When you get to your first flag, turn around and look down the row of flags.

If you have walked a straight line, all of the flags will be neatly lined up in a row. Congratulations! Or if you are like most people, the flags tend to be erratic and curve off to the left or right or both. In some cases this can be as much as 10 to 15 yards off line or in our case off track. Although you may not feel that a curve in your track will be important, the dog will correctly follow the curve and you may pull him off track in an attempt to make him track straight. This will only confuse the dog and frustrate you.

A simple trick to avoid this curve is to plant a flag in the ground and another one about 10 yards away. Now, walk approximately 100 yards away and turn around. Move either left or right until the two original flags line up. Now plant a third flag next to your left foot and walk straight towards the two flags (keeping them lined up), planting a flag next to your left foot every 10 yards. When you finish, all of your flags should be lined up in a row.

☐ **Locating Two Objects In Your Path**

Similar to the demonstration above, select two objects along the line you wish to lay the track. These could be a small tree and a telephone pole, a sign and a street light or just two trees. The items you select must be distinguishable and identifiable at a glance as your selected objects. It is easier to select a lone tree than the tallest tree in a stand of trees. In VST, you will be utilizing objects such as the corners of buildings, hedges, light poles, flag poles, fences, manhole covers, hedges, windows or doors on buildings, etc.

Once you locate these objects, write them down *AND* draw a small picture of them in a straight line from your current position on your map.

☐ **Start Flag and Articles**

In VST, there is only one flag, the starting flag. Start your leg by drawing the location of the start flag. Mark the location of each turn with a small picture or graphic to symbolize the turn. Mark each change of surface on your map. Record on each leg the number of yards of vegetated and non-vegetated surfaces by noting them as 20V (20 yards on vegetated surface) or 35N (35 yards on non-vegetated surface). Add the exact location of each article and note the location of buildings, sidewalks, ramps, streets, etc. on your map.

☐ **Landmarks**

Landmarks are objects or features of the terrain which you will use to locate the direction of the leg. A landmark can be anything which will not move and can be readily identifiable again. In VST, you will be utilizing objects such as the corners of buildings, hedges, light poles, flag poles, fences, manhole covers, hedges, windows or doors on buildings, etc.

☐ **Ground Markers**

Ground markers are objects or ground features along the track which will allow you to pinpoint the exact location of a start, turn, article, etc. Ground markers do not need to be a permanent feature, however it may be impossible to re-create your map at a later date using only ground markers. Remember, grass is mown, dirt spots grow weeds and flowers may die or wilt in only a few days. Paper bags, trash cans, automobiles and brush piles seem to mysteriously move or disappear in a relatively short time span. In VST we tend to use manhole covers, light poles, stripes in parking lots, etc. as our ground markers.

☐ **Compass Headings**

A compass heading will provide an easily re-layable leg and provide easy directions regardless of visibility or time. Identify the two objects or landmarks and using your compass, take a reading of the direction. Write down the direction (compass reading in degrees) and the approximate distance to the landmarks or objects on your map next to the specific leg.

☐ **Distance**

In addition to all of the above information, your map must contain distance markers for each leg. As you walk the leg, count your steps and using the conversion for your stride, mark down the yardage for each leg. As you lay your track, you will identify and locate landmarks and ground markers along the way. Draw a small picture of the object and write the distance to it on your map. An example would be if you are walking the first leg from the starting flag and at 45 yards the ground cover changes from short grass to mulch you would draw a line _____ across the leg line to designate a change in ground cover and note cover change to pavement 45V next to it and the surface type under the yardage. Adding these items on your map will make your map easier to follow and will increase your confidence when you are following the handler and the dog.

In VST, you will mark down all changes in surface. On a start leg of 150 yards followed by a turn, it might appear on your map in a form similar to the following diagram.

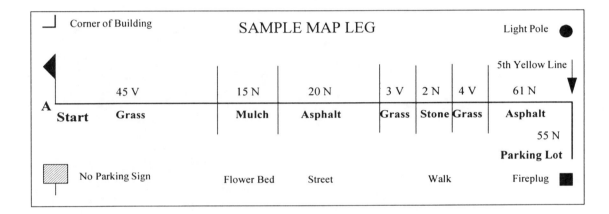

☐ **Time**

Always note the time you started laying the track and the time you completed it. The elapsed time from the time you started until the time the dog started is the age of the track. If you did not write down when you started, you will not know how old the track is.

☐ **Weather Conditions**

Note the weather conditions at the time you lay the track. If it is dry and windy, or cold and raining it will affect the tracking by the dog. Changes in temperature, wind, wind direction, time of day or other weather features will allow you to follow the progress of your dog in tracking. If it seem that the dog always has problems in the heat or cold, your records of previous tracks should verify this and allow you to work in these conditions to train your dog.

☐ **Ground Conditions**

Similar to weather conditions, ground conditions can effect tracking. Record whether the ground is dry, wet, damp with dew, dusty or if there is standing water on the track from previous or current weather conditions. Your records of previous tracks should document this and allow you to work in similar conditions again if required.

☐ **Day or Night**

Record whether you laid and ran this track during the day or at night.

PHOTO BY CHRISTY BERGEON

SAMPLE TRACKING CHART

Track _____ Event _____ Date _____

		V	N
N W			

Total Yardage		Tracklayer	
TL Start Time		Handler	
DOG Start Time		Dog Name	
Track Aging Time		Breed/Sex	
Ground Conditions		Articles	1. 2.
Weather Conditions			3. 4.
Wind Speed		Surfaces	1. 2.
Day/Night			3. 4.

Chapter 11

Choosing A Training Area

Land Requirements

"In Variable Surface Tracking, Judges, exhibitors, spectators and test giving clubs should be aware that these areas may be heavily used by the general public and accordingly, must make every effort to cooperate with these public areas and the people who use them in order to ensure that these variable surface tracking sites will continue to be available for future tests. Clubs and exhibitors alike must try to confine "exercise areas" for dogs to a small designated area and be sure that those areas are cleaned up before the test is over and the area is left in the same condition as it was at the start of the test, not only to promote responsible dog ownership but to promote good relations with the general public."

and

"In the case of Variable Surface Tracking, for the safety of the dog and handler, Judges must be cognizant of surface temperatures in hot weather, especially on asphalt and concrete. Tracks shall not be run on surfaces where the Judges and/or tracking committee have knowledge of recent treatment with chemicals that might cause an injury to the dog and handler. If conditions are such as to be unsafe for the dog and handler, the test shall be delayed, postponed or canceled..."

In training for Variable Surface Tracking your land requirements will be sufficiently different from TD or TDX work. As the intent of VST is to be performed in an "urban" environment, most of your training should be geared to areas such as school yards, parks, parking lots, business parks, malls, colleges and universities.

In VST, there are no "*clean*" fields or areas to train in. The purpose of the training is to acquaint your dog with heavily contaminated areas similar to those you would expect to find in a test location.

To train properly for VST, it will be best if you can locate four primary training areas.

□ **Business Park or Campus Facility**

One or more training areas such as business parks or campus facilities. We have had minimal difficulty in receiving permission to train on private property after explaining to the management, landlord or security personnel what our training methods encompassed and how we would be using the facility.

Try to select training areas which will be similar to test sites. In using this workbook, you will be attempting to overlay the specific components onto your facility. A training site with multiple buildings, walks, curbs, parking lots, grass and mulch areas will be suitable for many of the components.

□ **Retail Centers**

A Wal-Mart or Costco-type parking lot is suitable for teaching the transition components and introducing your dog to starts and legs on non-vegetated surfaces.

□ **Public Schools**

Try to have at least one public school in your list of training areas. The access to soccer, football or baseball fields, tennis courts, parking areas, fences and multiple buildings in a small area is extremely useful for helping your dog work in high contamination areas, around people, distractions and swirling scent.

□ **Parking Garage**

When we started this training program we had not seen a test with a leg through a parking garage we trained for the possibility of a parking garage being deemed as an open structure. We utilize parking garages to work on open building, ramp and stair components and if necessary as a primary training facility during extremely inclement weather. Were we ever glad we practiced in a garage when one of our VST tracks ended inside a garage! It may be possible to locate a suitable parking garage at your primary business park or campus facility.

Training in Contamination

School yards, parks, parking lots, business parks, colleges and universities are great places to introduce your dog to working in contaminated areas. When we are laying track or running our practice tracks we cannot control the general public and therefore we must train our dogs to expect to be greeted or have their tracking interrupted by people along the track. At each of the VST workshops I attended, John Barnard told us to expect someone to walk out of a building or get out of a car and come nose to nose with our dog. At our workshop in Houston we were introduced to this problem when two gentlemen tried to exit a building and found a 100+ pound Rottweiler blocking the doorway while searching for his track. The gentlemen, deciding that retreat was the best form of valor, decided to stay inside the building and wait for the dog and handler to move.

During a workshop at a college in El Paso, students from the college were exiting the main building when they came face to face with a Springer working his track. The handler stopped the dog and the students petted him before continuing on their way. After seeing these examples of what could happen, we wanted to be prepared for a similar situation to occur on our tracks in a test.

We have found that school grounds work wonders to help a dog become accustomed to distractions and multiple restarts. We have several elementary and junior high schools within a two or three mile area of our homes. One of our preparations for a test is to plan several afternoons when we can lay a short, 200 to 300 yard, track and then run it when school is out at 2:45. Talk about distractions, try 300 to 400 screaming kids who all want to pet the dog and ask you what you are doing! The first few time can be rather traumatic for both the handler and the dog. We don't worry about the dog staying *on* the track and there are no articles. Well, there were at first, but the kids kept picking them up. I do watch the dogs reaction and inter-reaction with the students, teachers and security. Most of these type tracks are run with from 15 minutes to 2 hours of age.

Be sure to go in and talk with the Principal and Security before you lay a track at a school. Security around schools is efficient and the safety of the children is paramount with the administration. We have used seven schools in this area and have not had a single principal say no after a brief conversation to explain what we wanted to do and after letting the principal meet our dogs. Don't do this cold, your dog must be extremely comfortable in tracking in heavily contaminated areas and around a lot of people. To work your dog up to this, walk them on a leash through the crowd a few times when school is starting or ending or lay a few tracks at night, or on the weekends to introduce your dog to the area.

We find the additional preparation for this potential problem paid off. On the first leg of one track the dog was approached by a woman and child who were crossing a parking lot to enter a county jail facility. The child walked up, hugged and petted the dog. When the woman and child left, the dog continued on his track, to his title. On another track, the dog was confronted on the next to the last leg by an elderly woman in a wheelchair who wanted to pet her. After the woman was asked to leave the tracking area by one of the judges, the dog continued down the track to her title.

PHOTO BY CHRISTY BERGEON

Chapter 12

Leads and Lead Handling

PHOTO BY ED PRESNALL

Using the right lead

Our training program is based on keeping the handler ten (10) feet from the dog as much of the time as possible. For this reason, we do not allow students to use any lead longer than 20 feet in length. The closer you are to the dog, the more confidence you will instill in the dog. During the initial first few weeks of introducing non-vegetated surfaces to your dog, it will be much easier for you to help your dog and keep it closer to the track if you are only a few feet away from it.

☐ **6-foot leather or nylon lead**

Start your training procedure with a 6-foot lead. Your initial training will begin with introducing *transition* areas into normal vegetated legs.

Working with a short lead will increase your ability to keep the dog on track when facing the transition from vegetated to non-vegetated surfaces or introducing starts on non-vegetated surfaces.

☐ **20-foot woven cloth or nylon lead**

Move to a 20-foot lead as your dog is progressing in its confidence on transitions from vegetated to non-vegetated surfaces or starts on non-vegetated surfaces. We utilize a two colored 20 foot lead for our training purposes. The first 10 feet of the lead is one color and the last 10 feet is another.

In training, it becomes quite easy for the handler to glance at the lead and know whether they are too far away from the dog or whether the dog is casting an excessive amount at a turn. This is a training and conditioning tool. We do not recommend that you use the two color lead in test situations, as the regulations state that the lead does not need to be marked at 10 foot. We utilize in a test situation, a color coordinated combination of collar, harness and solid color lead for each dog.

PHOTO BY CHRISTY BERGEON

☐ **Follow Your Dog**

One of the reasons we insist on using 20-foot leads is to allow the handler to follow their dog as it learns to discriminate between the track and scent problems around the track. A 20-foot lead will allow your dog to work an area approximately six yards wide on either side of the track. This area is wide enough to allow your dog to learn to solve problems yet will keep him within or near the scent cone of the track.

We have found that using a 30 or 40-foot lead allows the dog too much leeway to check out *interesting* places and tends to condition him to work well outside of the scent cone. The diagrams below visually display the difference in working your dog on a 20-foot *vs.* 40-foot lead. Teaching your dog to stay close to or in the scent cone will allow him to quickly assimilate the various surfaces and complete the component training at a much faster pace.

The following two diagrams are a visual representation of how far a dog can get off-track, based on the length of the lead.

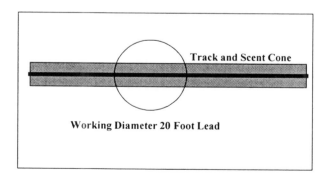

Working Diameter 20 Foot Lead

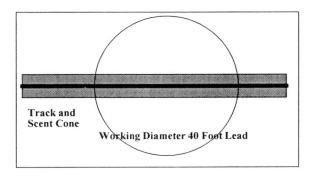

Working Diameter 40 Foot Lead

□   **The Visual Dog**

Every dog we have introduced to VST work has become extremely *visual* in their ability to spot trash or potential articles on non-vegetated surfaces at extreme distances. You will find that you need to allow your dog to inspect the potential article, disregard it, and then return to tracking. Pulling your dog off the potential article or refusing to go with him to inspect it can cause confusion and will increase your training time. These visual sightings and the subsequent following of the dog by the handler, have been stated as resembling watching a group of drunks stagger across a parking lot.

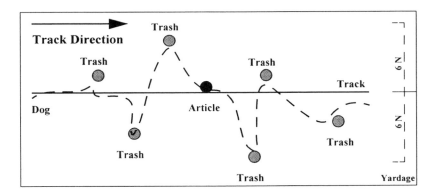

The Visual Dog

One of your jobs as a handler is to remain on the track and talk to your dog as he makes these brief off track excursions. The dog must be taught to investigate anything that could be an article, yet quickly discriminate between trash and articles and return to the track to continue tracking.

☐ *Note:* When working in *urban* environments, expect at some point for your dog to identify dead animals, birds, reptiles or rodents along the track. All manner of creature seems to have been run over in one or more of the large areas we train in. Although this can be a serious distraction to some dogs, we have been presented snakes, squirrels and birds as *potential articles* or *precious treasures* by our dogs along the way. Work with your dog and develop some form of a *leave it* command and a strong *restart* or *get back to work* command.

If your dog insists on investigating a *potential article* which is outside of the range of your 20-foot lead, you must be prepared to go with him *and* at the same time, remember exactly where you were on the track. Should the potential article your dog is investigating turn out to be trash, it is now your job to work with your dog to get him to return to the last known position on the track so that he may continue.

We call the process of remembering your place on the track **handler positioning**.

When you are following your dog, be aware of your surroundings. Look for landmarks, trees, light poles, manhole covers, etc. to position yourself along the track. In training, your tracklayer will know exactly where the track is or if you laid the track yourself, you should, however, look, look and look. Do not get complacent or comfortable watching your dog. Know your position to the track at all times. Tracking is a *team* sport, and in VST it will take both team members working together to be successful.

Using the diagram below, the potential landmarks or positioning tools have been identified to give you a better example of what handler positioning is all about and how you can use it to your advantage.

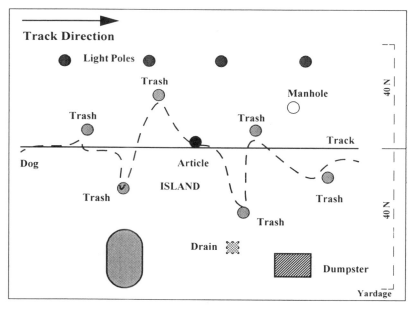

Handler Positioning

By locating landmarks as you navigate your track, you will have the added advantage of being able to back up or follow your dog back to the track. There is nothing more frustrating that following your dog off-track as he checks out an alleyway, curb or piece of trash and to suddenly realize that you have no idea where your dog was *on*-track. As you work your tracks, try to position landmarks in your mind which will allow you to be a supportive part of your team.

☐ **Carrying A Spare Lead**

As strange as it might sound, we've seen more tangled and broken leads when working in VST than in either TD or TDX work. Leads tend to get tangled in hedges, caught on fences or under automobile tires. We always recommend that you carry an additional 20-foot lead in your belt bag just in case yours is tangled or broken on the track.

PHOTO BY ED PRESNALL

Chapter 13

Motivation

Motivation

VST training is hard, exhaustive and mentally taxing work for your dog. As you work your dog you will notice days when he simply is not interested in tracking farther, appears bored with tracking or is approaching burn-out.

If your dog is having difficulty with one component, do not continually train on that specific component with the concept that we will do it until it is done right. Keeping your dog challenged and happily involved in the problem solving process is what your efforts should be directed towards. Select another component to work on, perhaps not so challenging, or include one of these motivational ideas into your practice session.

☐ **The Drag**

> For starting a dog out on non-vegetated surfaces we attach a sock or glove to a six foot lead. Walking the training leg in a normal manner, we drag the sock or glove behind us along the track. This method will lay down additional scent on the track and will make it easier for your dog to understand that the track continues or starts on a non-vegetated surface.

> We implement this concept when introducing transition areas, starts on non-vegetated surfaces and occasionally just to get the dogs attention on more advanced training tracks. When this idea is implemented on multiple component training tracks in a specific area, you should be able to see your dog track truer and closer to the track when he enters the *special* area.

> You may utilize this idea on any surface when starting a new dog instead of or in addition to one of the other motivational items lead the dog down the track.

☐ **Hide 'n Seek**

In many cases, the handler working the dog is the only person that ever works the dog. By allowing someone else to work your dog is beneficial to both the dog in introducing another variable into the tracking equation and to the handler. It is a chance when you can watch your dog from a distance, and in many cases, pick up on some small indication your dog may be making at a turn or transition that you may not see from your normal position behind the dog.

One method we use to excite the dogs is to have the handler lay a short track and hide at the end with an article. The person laying the track can hide behind a automobile, fence or wall, around the corner of a building or over the top of a berm. Try to locate a hiding place where you will be able to see the dog working the track. Normally we only lay a long "L" from 100-150 yards in length.

Have the person who will be handling the dog take it to a position behind the start. Stand at the start and drop the start article. Turn and wave or talk to your dog as you lay the track. Along the way, drop several additional articles. Once you have turned the corner or are out of the dogs sight, have the handler start preparing the dog. Put on the harness, walk to the start and tell the dog to *track* or *find mom/dad*.

Most dogs are so excited about tracking their owner that they must be restrained from running down the track and ignoring the additional articles. Have the handler work with the dog to stop and indicate each article. Restarting the dog to find you should not be a problem. You can implement this idea on vegetated or non-vegetated surfaces or integrate a transition area to help your dog. Two examples are shown below.

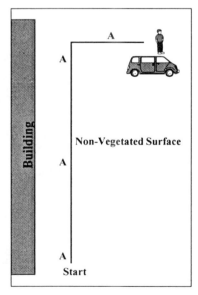

Hide 'n Seek
Hiding Behind A Car

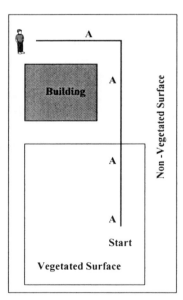

Hide 'n Seek
Behind A Building

☐ **Random Jackpots**

If your dog is food motivated or if you are having difficulty with article indication, place random jackpots of food at articles. In certain parts of the country, due to ants and other critters, it is almost impossible to leave any food on the track or at articles. In these cases, we carry the food and select one article at which the dog has made a good indication and make a spontaneous jackpot. Our objective is to keep the dog searching for articles with the opportunity to sparingly jackpot a quality indication or difficult article placement.

☐ **Favorite Toys**

Randomly, every 2 or 3 tracking sessions, replace one of the articles on the track with your dogs favorite toy. This will, like jackpots of random food on articles, keep him guessing and motivate him to find every article.

☐ **The Throw-Down**

In no situation is the dog allowed to leave the tracking area when it is frustrated. Each tracking session must end on a high note and a good find for the dog. To assure ourselves of this, we always carry an extra leather article and a small dog biscuit or two. If the dog becomes frustrated working on a component and we do not think we can motivate the dog to continue tracking, we immediately toss out or throw-down the spare article and allow the dog to find it. He receives an immediate praise and a small food jackpot for his efforts and our tracking day is over.

This is a difficult concept for most people to grasp. After all, you have just laid a track and aged it when suddenly your dog is confused, frustrated or simply will not track. The natural tendency is to push or force the dog through the remainder of the track. It is possible to damage your dogs confidence in tracking by continuing on when it is obvious that the dog is not going to track.

PHOTO BY ED PRESNALL

Chapter 14

Getting Started

PHOTO BY ED PRESNALL

"Handlers have the responsibility to train and prepare the dog for a variety of terrain and conditions which may be encountered in a Tracking Test. It is essential for handlers to realize that obstacles are an important characteristic of the TDX test and train the dog to work through obstacles of varying difficulty."

"In Variable Surface Tracking, although there are no physical obstacles as found in TDX, handlers must train for all types of conditions and surfaces that might be commonly found in a variable surface tracking area, such as soft and hard dirt, blacktop, concrete, paving materials, sand, gravel, wood chips or metal stairs and to train for the diverse scenting conditions that exist in variable surface tracking."

Introducing Your Dog To Non-Vegetated Surfaces

☐ When starting a dog out on NV surfaces, it is not necessary to stamp and/or scuff the NV surface. Scent may be affected by heat and as such any additional scuffing or dragging of your feet may change the chemical balance of the scent.

☐ Walk normally to the start. Stand calmly for about 10-15 seconds facing the direction of the first leg of the track. Take a deep breath and step normally down the first leg. Stop every 3 to 5 steps at first and bend over and place your hand flat on the surface. This will leave a small amount of body oil from your hand on the track. If laying a track next to a building or fence it is advantageous to drag a glove down the building wall or fence to leave extra scent for the dog.

☐ It is not necessary to double or triple lay starts or corners. Such actions could be confusing to the dog, in principal what we are trying to enforce is that the track has a direction and it is the dogs responsibility to determine the direction and follow the scent pads throughout the track.

If you feel it is necessary to lay down additional scent at starts or turns, drag a sock or glove behind you when walking that part of the track. Review Chapter 13, *Motivation*, for more information on this technique.

☐ When training for a variable surface test, you will be running your dog in areas which have a scent from numerous other people. This means that your dog must be able to discriminate between the scent of the tracklayer and others who have walked across your track. There are several ways to introduce your dog to this concept.

One of the easiest is to have two people lay a track by walking side by side. One of the tracklayers will leave an article at the start to allow the dog to be provided with the scent of the person he is to follow. After 50 yards, the two tracklayers will stop, with one facing left and one right and continue on in a "T" pattern. This intersection or corner must not be marked. Each person walks away from the other, and the tracklayer the dog is to follow (tracklayer #1) leaves an ending article after another 50 yards.

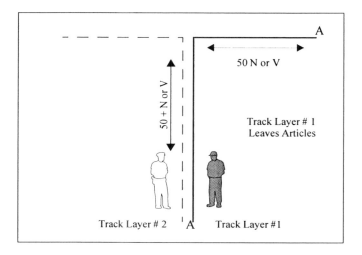

The Double T

Start this type of training on a vegetated surface to introduce your dog to close proximity contamination. Several people who have been training for VST have said that their dogs seem to have problems when the "cross tracks" or contamination is parallel to the track. This exercise will help condition your dog to that possibility and should enhance his ability to stay on-track.

As you work through the Chapter on *Transition Components*, return to this example and utilize a 15 or 20 yard start on vegetated surface with a transition to non-vegetated for the remainder of the exercise. When you are satisfied that your dog can perform this type of scent discrimination in transition areas, relocate the track so that the entire track is on non-vegetated surface.

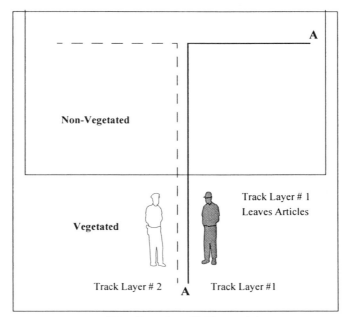

The Double T Transition

◆   In your training, you can insert this exercise as a motivational item for your dog at any point in your training process to break up the somewhat tedious process of only running your dog on components or training tracks.

PHOTO BY CHRISTY BERGEON

Tracking to a corner on asphalt

☐ **Intersecting Stair Step Tracks**

Another training method to employ to enhance scent discrimination with your dog is to lay two tracks in an intersecting stair step pattern. Start this type of training on a vegetated surface to introduce your dog to close proximity contamination. As the tracks cross each other, a scenting problem will face your dog. Work with your dog at these points until he is confident in remaining on the track.

As you can see in the following diagram, the legs of the two tracks intersect each other, offering multiple scenting problems on the same track. This training method is usually employed to additionally enhance your dogs concentration by running two dogs at the same time. Additionally, you could utilize several other people to walk the second track as you and your dog ran the first one or have one or two people walk between the tracks diagonally as a distraction. At the point the people reach a dog running on the track, they should stop the handler, pet the dog and the allow the handler to restart the dog while they continue on.

This exercise will build concentration around distractions. If the individual legs are long enough between the turns, a third track could be inserted at a diagonal splitting the other two tracks and adding additional distractions. You must utilize legs long enough for the dogs to not to be able to air-scent the next leg. We normally use legs of 60 yards which we increase to 90 or even 100 yards on a windy day.

As you work through the Chapter on Transition Components, return to this example and utilize a 15-20 yard start on vegetated surface with a transition to non-vegetated for the remainder of the exercise. When you are satisfied that your dog can perform this type of scent discrimination in transition areas, relocate the track so that the entire track is on non-vegetated surface.

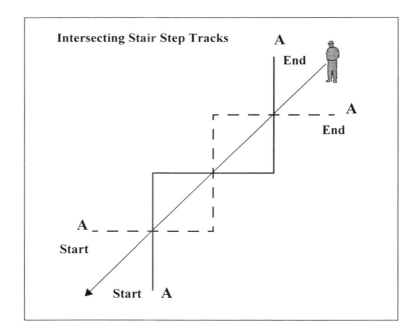

❑   **The Start**

From the Regulations "*The start and the first fifteen (15) yards of the track shall be in an area of vegetation and shall have one flag at the beginning which permits the track to go in one of several possible directions within an arc of 180 degrees, whenever possible ...*

With the majority of dogs failing at the start or on the first leg, a strong start is imperative to your success. Do not gloss over or assume your dog can perform consistent starts when training your dog for VST.

Since your start will be in a vegetated area, train for starts on grass. The Chapters 17 Transition *Components* and Chapter 18 *Start Components* are designed to help you work your dog and yourself through the most difficult portion of the track.

As you lay your tracks, remember that your start leg can *go in one of several possible directions within an arc of 180 degrees*. Bring your dog to the start from different directions and allow the dog to *problem solve* the direction of the track. Continually working your dog by bringing them directly to the track or facing the direction of the start leg will neither train your dog to problem solve nor enhance your ability to pass at a test.

On at least one training session each month, we spend the entire session laying varying starts and short L's. This break in our training allows our dogs to become competent and sure of themselves at starts and increases their motivation to track.

PHOTO BY CHRISTY BERGEON

☐ **Training For The Start**

The most critical portion of any track is the start. This is not a race. A few extra seconds at the start will allow you to be better prepared for what will come farther down the leg or around the next turn. Take your time, do not rush, for once your dog has passed the start flag there is no opportunity to restart.

The Regulations state: *At the start of the track, the dog is to be given ample time to take the scent and to begin tracking. The handler may use any method provided no force, guidance or roughness is used to start the dog at the starting flag. Since there is no second flag, the handler must wait for the dog to commit itself before leaving the starting flag. Once the dog has left the starting flag, the test has begun and no restart is permitted.*

Work slowly and calmly at the start. We prefer to walk the dog near the start flag, down, sit or stand the dog in or near the scent pad and article and then put on the harness. This extra time at the start allows you to calmly evaluate the surroundings and prepare yourself for the track while your dog acquires enough scent from the scent pad and article to successfully discriminate the tracklayers scent from other scents in the area.

The Regulations state: *The handler may pick up the article at the starting flag and use it, as well as subsequent articles, to give scent to the dog while on the track.*

Take every advantage. Pick up the article and carry it with you. The longer the track and the more non-vegetated surface you work, the more you will find yourself re-scenting your dog.

PHOTO BY ED PRESNALL

The Regulations state: *The handler will work no closer than 10 feet from the dog."*

Once again, use the regulations to your benefit. Stay close to your dog. It will help to keep him close to the track in training while building his confidence.

☐ **Non-Vegetated Starts**

We implement a series of procedures to introduce a dog to non-vegetated surfaces. Each of these examples will utilize a short "L" track with a 30 to 50 yard start leg and a 20 to 30 yard second leg as shown in the figure below.

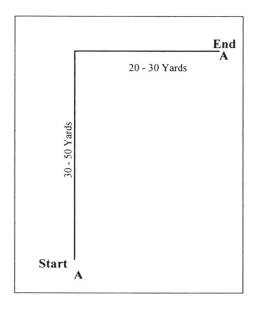

You will want to implement this introduction exercise on each of the following surfaces:

- Asphalt
- Concrete
- Dirt
- Brick
- Mulch
- Gravel
- Stone
- Along Curbs

PHOTO BY ED PRESNALL

To use this exercise as a *transition component,* start the exercise on a non-vegetated surface and end it on grass.

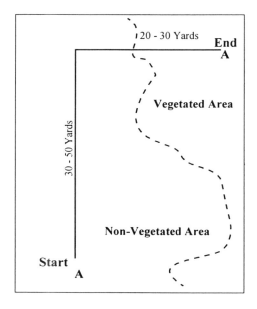

Normally we will lay three or four such exercises during a given training session and end the training. This concept will instill a desire for your dog to *want* to track and will keep him excited about working the next time you practice.

♦ When training, you can insert this exercise as a motivational item for your dog at any point in your training process to break up the somewhat tedious process of continually running your dog on components or training tracks.

Transitioning from asphalt to grass

PHOTO BY ED PRESNALL

□   **Blind Starts**

Once your dog is consistently selecting the proper direction for the start, you might try to implement the following method for "unknown" starts to plot the start and first leg.

□   **Searching for the Start**

Unmarked starts may be utilized to increase your dogs awareness of the track direction. Rather than having your start article at the flag, have your tracklayer toss the start article off to the side about 6-10 feet from the start flag.

Take your dog to the article and allow him to stand, sit or down at the article. When your normal time spent at the scent pad is completed, tell him to find the track.

Once your dog can locate and follow the track when it does not begin at a start flag, he should be able to consistently perform clean starts from the flag. This exercise will also assist your dog in recovering when it overshoots a corner or loses the track along the way.

As your dog progresses, expand the circle from 6-10 feet out to about 20 yards.

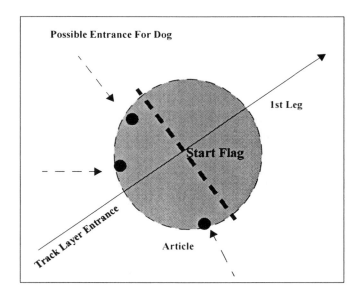

□   **Article Indication**

In VST, article indication must be solid. With many articles appearing to be trash, your dog must learn to discriminate between actual articles and trash on the track. Whether your dog's form of indication is a stand, sit or down does not matter. The regulations state only that the dog must *indicate* the article, a loosely defined statement which normally means that the handler returned with the article.

If the dog indicates something, even if you think it is not an article, move up the line and look. Unless you are sure it is not an article, pick it up, hold it overhead to display to the judges or your tracklayer that your dog has found and indicated an object and put it in your bag. It is always easier to return with too many articles rather than sheepishly stare off into the distance as the judge explains that your dog stopped at an article, but you did not investigate.

One of the easiest methods we have developed to work on article indication has the added benefit of also teaching two other fundamental components of VST tracking.

This procedure has three basic configurations for use in your training site. Lay a long "L" track for your dog. We have found that it is preferable to utilize leg lengths of at least 100-150 yards. As your dog progresses, you may want to extend these leg lengths to as much as 300 yards. We utilize a program of reinforcement of article indication using this method two times-a-week for a period of four weeks.

Along both legs of the "L" place articles every 10 or so yards. On a 150 yard leg, you will have a start article and then 10 or more additional articles, a turn and starting ten yards after the turn you will have another 10 or more articles.

As shown in the diagram below, start with the track being laid on grass. Allow the track to age from 30 minutes to one hour and run the dog. As the dog reaches and indicates an article, reinforce your preferred method of indication. Praise your dog for the indication. If you prefer to utilize food in your training, you may give your dog a single piece of food or kibble at each article. Restart your dog and repeat your praise and reinforcement at every article. At the final article, reward your dog with praise and let him know that he has performed well.

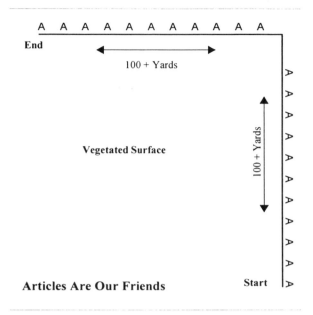

A A A A A A A A A A A

End

◄——————————►

100 + Yards

Vegetated Surface

100 + Yards

Articles Are Our Friends   **Start**

After your dog has successfully completed this track several times, the article indication should be developing into a standard "known" action while the restart after the article should be filled with excitement at the dogs ability to return to tracking.

Now relocate the track so that only the starting leg is on grass, as displayed on the next page. Normally we utilize a 15-20 yard grass start. The balance of the first leg and all of the second leg will be laid in the parking lot.

Repeat the above procedure. At first you may need to help your dog locate and navigate the turn to the second leg. If your assistance is required to locate this turn, remain standing facing the direction of the first leg. Allow your dog to search for the turn. When he locates it, praise him and step quickly to follow him down the next leg

PHOTO BY CHRISTY BERGEON

Article Indication

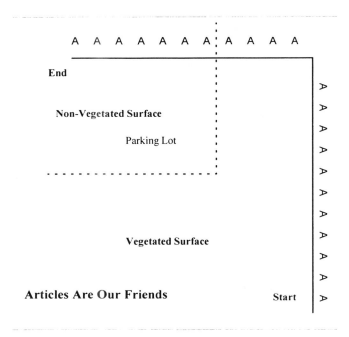

When your dog is successfully executing this configuration of the track, reduce the number of articles on the track by one half, see the figure below, and repeat the procedure.

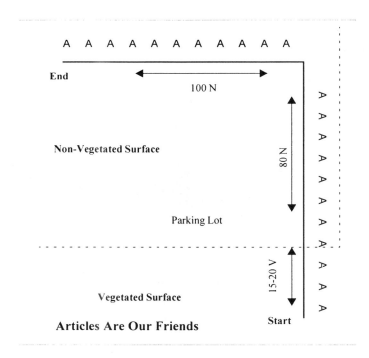

By this time, through the use of operative conditioning, you should have a steady, article conscious, easily restarted dog which is confident in tracking short distances on both grass and non-vegetated surfaces.

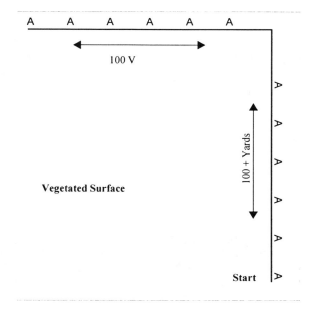

Now re-lay the same track utilizing only one or two articles on each leg. After your dog has executed this procedures two or three times, he should be confident in indicating articles, restarts and best of all, locating and navigating a turn on a non-vegetated surface.

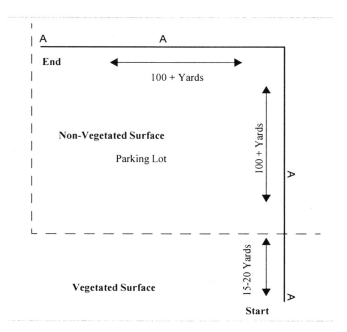

☐ **TRANSITION AREAS**

Seemingly one of the hardest things for a dog to accomplish is to consistently remain on track when changing from vegetated to non-vegetated surfaces. Some of the various transition areas you may face will be:

☐ **Streets**

Street-crossings are the most common form of transition on a VST track. Unlike TDX tracking where for years we have taught our dogs to search for the tracklayer's scent across the road, you will need to work with your dog on searching for the scent on the non-vegetated surface.

Your dog will react differently to streets with curbs and gutters than it will to a grade level street crossing. The height difference between the curb and the street will allow the scent to be drawn along the curb to the left and right of the track. Encourage your dog to search the curbs and to determine the actual direction of the tracklayer's footsteps across the road.

PHOTO BY ED PRESNALL

Transitioning a parking lot to a curb

⌘ **Hint:** When laying the transition track, reach down and place your hand flat against the curb as you cross the street. This will place a small amount of your body oil on the curb and will help you dog in locating the exact transition point. Until your dog is confident in searching and tracking their way across a transition area, it may be necessary to stop every five or six steps and repeat the placing of your hand on the surface of the street.

On a grade level crossing, or a street without a curb, reach down and place your hand flat against the pavement as you cross the street. Again, it may be necessary until your dog is confident in searching and tracking their way across a transition area, it may be necessary to stop every five or six steps and repeat the placing of your hand on the surface of the street.

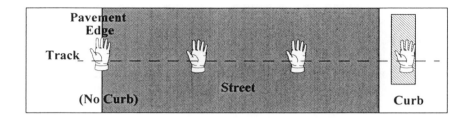

☐ **Dirt, Gravel, Mulch and Stone**

Transitions to dirt, gravel, mulch and stone are the easiest transitions we have seen our dogs progress through.

❖ Dirt, unless it is a very hard surface type hardpan, holds the scent in the indention of the footsteps. Hardpan tends to react more like asphalt (as defined below).

❖ Gravel due to the natural indentions of the smaller stones, or in the case of pea-gravel walks, the underlayment of grout between the stones, holds scent in a very specific footstep pattern.

❖ Mulch, almost a vegetated like surface tends to be the easiest of all surfaces for the dogs to master. The bark or shredded bark holds the scent on the uneven surfaces and makes for fairly easy tracking by most dogs. We try to implement as much mulch as possible with all of our starting or beginner dogs to help build their confidence on a new surface.

❖ Stones, depending upon their size offer few training problems for most dogs. The normal size found in our area ranges from 1-2 inch stones, typically laid in a 2-3 inch deep walkway or landscape border. The natural indentions between the stones holds the scent in a modified footstep pattern. One of the interesting things that we found in training dog on stones is that many dogs require multiple introductions to them to be comfortable with the sound the stones make when walked across.

☐ **Brick**

Unusual in its texture, brickwork tend to hold scent in random patterns. The typical surface of brick is rough and grasps the scent in the footsteps, however, the scent which is dispersed from the tracklayer tends to be held in the indentions of the grout lines between the brick. You may see your dog working in a somewhat random pattern when first introduced to this surface. If you watch your dog closely, you will notice that he is more intent on searching the grout areas between the bricks, where the scent tends to collect, and not the individual footsteps on the bricks themselves.

⌘ **Hint:** When laying the transition track, use smaller or "baby" steps to cross the transition area. When you progress to larger areas (over 10 yards in width) it may be necessary to stop every five or six steps and place of your hand on the surface of the street as described in *Streets* above.

☐ **Asphalt**

Asphalt is where you will strive to have your dog comfortable. The vast majority of parking lots and large non-vegetated areas you will face during a test track will be on or near asphalt.

It is normally a petroleum-based product which is mixed with finely ground gravel. When a new parking lot has been paved, in many cases a petroleum-based top-coat or sealer is applied to reduce wear and increase the life-span of the parking lot. In many older parking lots (5+ years old) the original top coating has been worn off by vehicular traffic resulting in a cracking or crumbling of the surface which holds scent in a similar manner to that of finely ground gravel, sand or dirt.

PHOTO BY CHRISTY BERGEON

Tracking on Asphalt

■ **Note:** When working on an asphalt surface, remember that like other non-vegetated surfaces small changes in the surface height will collect scent. The painted stripes of a parking area will hold more scent than the asphalt surface itself.

☹ **Caution:** When working on new asphalt make sure there is not a coating or top-coat which might still be wet or emitting a chemical odor. Our rule of thumb when working with asphalt is that if we can smell any type of chemical smell or if the surface is oily to touch, we *do not* track on this surface.

On each type of asphalt, the transition from one type of non-vegetated surface, including the various types of asphalt, must be trained for as you would for any other transition area. Expect your dog to react during a transition from one surface type to another in a similar manner to a transition from vegetated to non-vegetated surfaces.

☐ **Concrete**

Concrete is used in different methods in many urban environments. The various surfaces of concrete hold scent in different methods and will require you to train your dog on each of the surfaces to be prepared for what you may find in training or on your test track.

Tracking on Concrete

❖ **Smooth Surface**

Typically found in parking garages. This surface is polished to a smooth finish for ease of cleaning and resistance to tire rubber, oil, antifreeze and other liquids from staining or being integrated with the surface of the garage floor. This surfaces holds little scent directly on the track itself and tends to allow the scent to flow across the floor and collect on painted parking lines, in corners and along the walls of the garage.

☹ **Caution:** When working your dog in parking garages, always watch for standing water or pools of liquids which could endanger your dog if ingested or may cause you or your dog to slip and fall.

❖ **Textured Surface**

In some areas, you will find that concrete has been utilized by the designers to create a faux brickwork or textured pattern to create an enhanced overall design to the project.

This surface tends to hold the scent in the small indentions created by the designer's pattern with some scent being held directly on the track itself due to the roughness of the surface.

❖ **Brush Finish**

One of the easiest non-vegetated surfaces for your dog to track on. The concrete is finished with workers utilizing large brushes to create a rough finish to the surface to enhance traction in cold or wet weather.

The finish, made up of thousands of tiny brush strokes, creates small indentions which hold the scent on the original track. Typically found in entrance ways, walks and loading docks around buildings where pedestrian traffic is expected.

❖ **Rough Laid**

A standard surface for many concrete parking lots, streets, esplanades, curbs and gutters, this surface holds scent in a manner similar to older asphalt.

On each type of concrete, the transition from one type of non-vegetated surface, including the various types of concrete, must be trained for as you would for any other transition area. Expect your dog to react during a transition from one surface type to another in a similar manner to a transition from vegetated to non-vegetated surfaces.

One method used on beginning transition areas with, our dogs is to locate one or more areas where we can plot the following type of transition track.

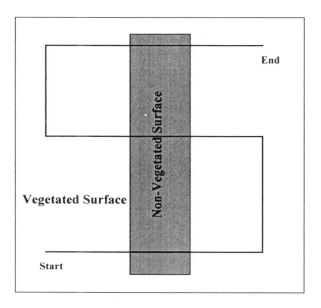

Using the above figure, you can use asphalt or concrete with its various surfaces, dirt, mulch, gravel or stone to simulate transition areas during training. Your objective is to have your dog work in a steady, on-track manner when entering and exiting the transition area.

When implementing the above example, do not use streets with curbs or gutters, as it will be an additional problem for your dog to work through. As your training progresses, you will integrate components which will include curbs and gutters to your training program.

Another example, shown in the figure below, introduces your dog to transition areas to increase your dogs ability to accommodate the introduction of multiple surface changes and types of variable surfaces into it's training program.

Strategically placing a generous amount of articles on each transition training tracks and components will assist the dog in confidently working on these new surfaces. As your dog progresses and its confidence in working in non-vegetated areas increases, reduce the number of articles used in a component until there is only a start and ending article.

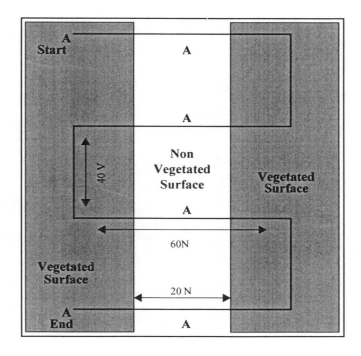

Working an asphalt surface

□ **Building Effect**

A building can effect your track by pulling or pushing the scent in an area equivalent to 3 times the height of the building. This type of effect is known as the *building shadow*. If your track is laid near a building which is 20-feet tall, the scent could be effected up to sixty feet, or more away.

This effect is emphasized more when wind is added to the equation. The wind tends to whip over and around the building, pushing the scent away from the track. In situations where the track runs between buildings, the scent can be pushed and pulled by wind currents, swirling the scent from the original track off of both of the buildings.

□ **Building Shadow**

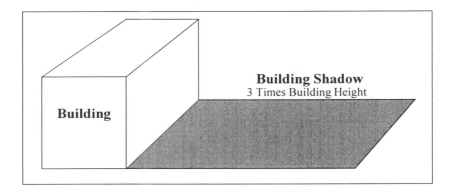

□ **Wind Effect (One Building)**

Depending upon the wind direction, the scent from the track may be pushed across the *building shadow* and away from the original track.

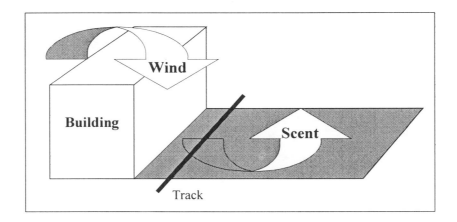

□ **Wind Effect (One Building)**

Or it could be pushed along or up over the building. In this situation, your dog will work much closer to the building.

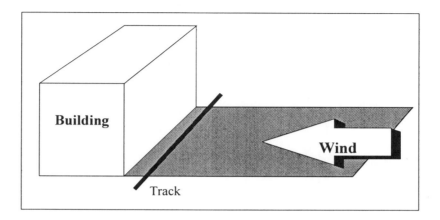

□ **Wind Effect (Multiple Buildings)**

When the track is laid between buildings you must be aware of the wind coming over the top of the buildings. The wind can create a swirling effect between the buildings disbursing the scent onto the buildings on both sides of the track. Your dog may alternatively work one building and then the other while trying to determine the location of the actual track.

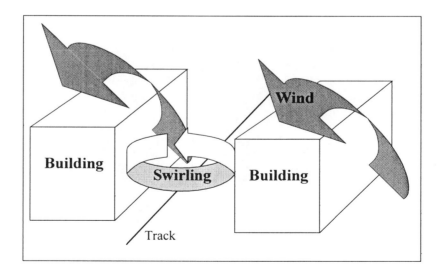

☐ **Wind Effect (Multiple Buildings)**

When the track is laid between buildings either into *or* with the wind, the building will create a tunnel effect, forcing your dog through the tunnel. Since your dog will be pushed through the tunnel by the scent, you must be very aware of any indication of a turn at *or* near the end of the tunnel. Most dogs in this situation will overshoot the turn and then indicate a loss of scent. Be prepared to work with your dog to back up to a point where your dog can once again *reestablish* contact with the track and slowly work through the turn.

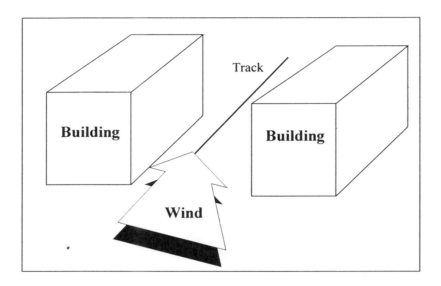

Working the side of a building

◻ **Variable Surface Tracking Myths**

Myth - *Your dog will hit a wall on the age of a track.*

Although some trainers have stated that their dogs reach a point where they can no longer track or even start regressing in their tracking abilities, utilizing random age while training for specific components seems to introduce the dogs to working on non-vegetated surfaces without regard to the age of the track.

Myth - *Fresh tracks on non-vegetated surfaces are easier for the dog than older tracks.*

In reality, we have found that time or age in VST works to your advantage. We start new VST dogs with tracks aged from 45 minutes to one hour, but rarely worry about whether the track is properly aged. In one session the tracks might be aged 45 minutes and the next session the age might be three hours.

It appears that as the scent disperses over time, the original footsteps are easier for the dog to follow. Evan an experienced TDX dog has an easier time negotiating non-vegetated surfaces when the tracks are aged several hours.

As we have stated before, VST is more mental than physical. Each of us that have worked in TDX carries extra mental baggage with us. We have a desire to slowly work up the age on a track to allow our dog to get used to the scent. In our training program we have found that once the handler gets over "*worrying*" about the age of the tracks, the dog works closer to the track and everyone seems to have more fun.

Myth - *You must have a TDX to work on Variable Surfaces.*

The first five dogs we have worked with utilizing this program have all been TD dogs. One received his title in nine months of training and two others succeeded in seven months. The dogs we are working with that currently have their TDX titles, the major problem is introducing them to transition areas, as most TDX dogs have been taught to *jump* across non-vegetated areas and search for the track on the other side.

PHOTO BY ED PRESNALL

□   **Training With Aged Tracks**

The following is a example of how we work in a training session when working on non-vegetated surfaces regarding the age of the tracks.

We train on a random pattern of age of the tracks. We do not want the dog to become dependent on a particular age of a track in order for him to perform. The average track we plot averages from one and one-half hours to four hours in age. Times have been added for your reference and do vary with each training session.

Pre-Tracklaying Discussion (5:30 P.M.)

We arrive at a training site and when everyone has assembled, we first discuss what we are going to do for each dog. If a dog is having problems with a specific component or if the handler is having problems under certain conditions, we try to utilize a component and area of the training site to support and work through those problems. We assign tracklayers for each dog or in the case of a new dog or a class of new dogs only the trainers lay the tracks while the handlers watch.

Tracklaying (6:00 P.M.)

The tracklayers go off to lay the individual tracks. In cases where we are working with advanced dogs, we will assign two tracklayers to lay a track with one of them leaving the articles.

If, for example, we have a beginner dog in the class, we will lay a series of transition components for the beginner dog. For the average dog, we will lay a series of components and for the advanced dog we will combine components to form a track.

Post-Tracklaying Discussion (7:00-8:00 P.M.)

The tracklayers have returned, we sit and discuss each track. We are trying to determine whether anything unusual happened while laying the track and learn specific challenges the dog may face on a given leg. Wind direction, freshly mown areas, heavy pedestrian traffic and article placement consumes much of this discussion. This can take from ten minutes to an hour, depending on the number of tracks that were laid and questions which were asked by the tracklayers and handlers.

Running Tracks (8:10-9:00 P.M.)

The first dog runs their first track. In this example, the first track is approximately two hours old. The other dogs follow in sequence, rotating the dogs to allow each of the dogs to rest between tracks. The final tracks are being run at approximately three and one-half to four hours of age. All other handlers, students and spectators follow each dog on each track. We maintain a distance ranging from 10 feet to 30 yards from the dog that is working.

Our distances from the working dog simulates what might happen in a test and allows the dog to become comfortable working in or near a crowd.

Post Track Discussion(10:00-11:00 P.M.)

Each handler discusses what they saw and learned on the track they ran. The trainers and other handlers offer suggestions, differing opinions and advice. We plan a proposed schedule of components to work on at the next training session.

As you can see, we spend almost as much time discussing what we are going to do, discussion of what we did and then critiquing each dog and handler team as we spend laying and running the tracks. The allocation of discussion time allow everyone to have input into the performance of each handler/team. Many times in these discussions the handler is given a different perspective of how their dog indicated a turn, article or a specific handling technique that allows the handler to become a more proficient part of the team.

PHOTO BY CHRISTY BERGEON

☐ **Night Tracking**

One of the nice things about training for VST is tracking at night. When you are training in business parks, schools or campus locations, you will find that they are both well lit and lightly traveled at night. Laying a track after work and running it after dark will help you maintain a structured tracking schedule and will be much cooler for you and your dog during hot summer months.

☺ **Advantages**

⌘ **Cooler Temperatures**

Depending on your work schedule, you can continue your tracking exercises through those hot summer or cold winter months.

⌘ **Less Automotive and Pedestrian Traffic**

Most training areas are deserted after dark.

⌘ **"Watching" the Building Effect**

When tracking at night, you can watch the effect a building has on your track. If it is hot outside and the building is air-conditioned, the building will push the scent away from the building. If it is cool outside and the building is heated, it will be pulled toward the building. This is readily prevalent around many glass buildings found in business parks and on campuses. By watching your dog follow a track a known distance from a building you can see these effects.

⌘ **Increased Article Indication**

Night tracking will force you to watch your dog's actions more closely, as you will not generally be able to see the articles. You will need to work on better article indication from your dog.

⌘ **"Known" Tracks Are "Blind" Tracks**

Even if you lay the track in daylight and draw a proper map, portions of your track will be "blind" to you due to the shadows, unlighted areas and buildings. This will help you to increase your ability to work closely with your dog as a team.

⌘ **More Security**

Mobile or walking security is normally increased in these locations after dark. In the areas we train in, we have become familiar with many of the security guards and they enjoy stopping by to watch our dogs work.

☹ **Disadvantages**

⌘ **It's Dark Out There**

Your tracks appear different after dark. Places you would think nothing about laying a track in, like an alleyway or behind a building, can become a dark forbidden area at night.

⌘ **Increased Caution Is Required**

In the dark, it is easy to step off a curb, or into a small hole in the grass and fall. Use caution when tracking around berms, hedges, curbs and gutters and related areas.

The automobile traffic which may be in the area will have a much more difficult time of seeing you and your dog. Watch carefully for moving traffic or appoint someone to be the safety director on all tracks. Do not hesitate to stop your dog and wait for moving traffic.

Pedestrians entering or leaving buildings can be easily startled if your dog suddenly appears from a shadow or around the corner of a building.

⌘ **More Security**

It's nice to know that security is always near, but security personnel can take up a lot of your time *if you allow it*. We try to meet with the security people who will be working on the nights we track and explain exactly what we are doing and that we have permission to be in the area. We have found that most security guards are *dog people* too and like to watch the dogs work and are willing to watch and then wait for our discussion periods to ask questions.

PHOTO BY CHRISTY BERGEON

Making a turn off of a berm in the dark

Chapter 15

Danger Areas

Caution !

Use caution while training for VST in parking lots, business parks or campus locations. You may come in contact with several substances which can become a hazard to you and your dog.

☐ **Liquids**
Antifreeze, coolant moisture, transmission fluid, road salts, oil or other chemicals may have leaked out of automobiles in the area. These may be extremely toxic to your dog if ingested. Liquids on the tracking surface can cause you or your dog to slip or fall.

☐ **Chemicals**
When working on VST, be aware of your surroundings. Watch for maintenance people who may be spraying with pesticides, fertilizers or other chemicals and *do not* track in that area until sufficient time has passed for the chemicals to be absorbed into the ground.

☐ **Traffic**
Always be alert for traffic. When possible, have your track layer or an additional person available to warn of moving or oncoming traffic. Don't be afraid to stop your dog, and wait on a vehicle or pedestrian traffic to pass.

Chapter 16

Track Components
The Building Blocks of VST

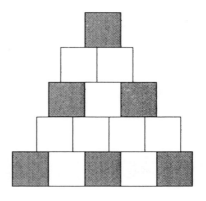

□ **Track Components**

The following diagrams have been taken from actual VST tracks. These components are the ***heart*** of our training program. Although many of the components appear similar, each one, treated as an exercise, will build a stronger foundation for you and your dog. They will introduce you to situations which can and have occurred in actual tests and increase your potential to pass in a VST test.

In the execution of most of these components, we add a start or ending leg or "L" to the exercise. The concept is to work on short, 150 to 250 yard training tracks and run two or three each time you train.

VST work requires intense concentration from your dog. It is a tiring and draining experience for your dog to successfully negotiate the components. Make sure your dog always ends the day on an emotional high, even if it means that you cut short a track or training session.

The end of every training session should be dedicated to a step by step discussion of each track. A frank review by your tracklayer and other trackers who may be present during handling and your dog's problem solving ability will allow you to see how your dog works from several points-of-view.

Many times, small problems, track indications or handler guiding is noticed first by the tracklayer or spectators and is pointed out in these discussions. Your opinion of how the dog solved the problems along with your handling skills or problems and what you felt was gained or lost by the experience should be openly discussed. If you are going to be a part of a *team* with your dog, you must understand what you see, and what others perceive is happening on the track. These discussions can be a wonderful learning tool.

We would advise that you first work through this workbook in Chapter order. One Chapter of *Components* at a time. Begin with ***Transitions and Starts***. You will find as you advance in your training, you can combine most of the starts and transitions examples with other components as you advance in your training.

Yardage, when offered on components, is for your benefit. It is derived from the actual tracks of the components. Adjust the component yardage to fit your training area.

Chapter 17

Transition Components

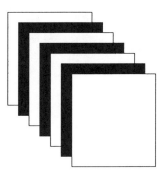

The ***Transition Components*** of VST training, and your ability to help your dog become comfortable with working in transition areas is one of the keys to becoming successful in working in VST.

In working with transition areas, consider that each area is similar to working in a TDX field where you are tracking through grass which is waist high when the cover changes and you are suddenly working in a 4 inch high mowed grass field. Your dog takes a moment to determine whether the track continues or turns, then progresses down the track.

In VST, the changes of cover or transition areas occur as you move to or from vegetated to non-vegetated surfaces. These transition areas may happen multiple times on a given leg, or may be dispersed throughout your track.

Allow your dog the time to evaluate this new surface and to check out the fringes of the transition area before continuing. As your dog gains confidence in working through these transition areas, you may see a different tracking style develop from vegetated to non-vegetated surfaces.

PHOTO BY ED PRESNALL

Transitioning from a grass berm into asphalt

Transition Components

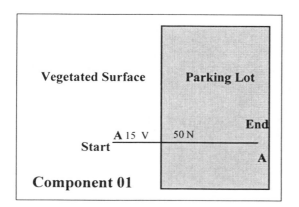

Component 01

(01) DIRECT TRANSITION

The basic component for all non-vegetated turns, and preparation for the ***moment of truth***, which you and your dog will face in a test. Practice this component over and over. Your dog must become proficient in continuing to track from the vegetated to the non-vegetated surface.

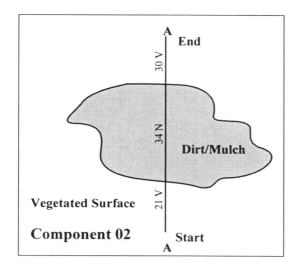

Component 02

(02) ACROSS DIRT/MULCH/GRAVEL

Transitions across dirt, mulch, gravel or stones should not be a difficult component for your dog to master.

Each of these surfaces holds scent much better than asphalt or concrete. We always try to allow the dog to work on these surfaces as often as possible to give it additional confidence and motivation.

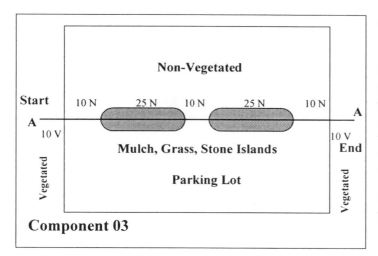

Component 03

(03) DIRT, MULCH OR STONE ISLANDS

In reality this is a combination of components, starting with vegetated to non-vegetated and working across the track on various surfaces until the track ends back on a vegetated surface. This is an easy component which will build confidence in your dog when working in transition areas.

Drop an article on each of the islands to further motivate your dog.

⌘ **Hint:** *When starting on transitions, work close to your dog. We recommend using a six foot lead for beginning the transition process and working up to a 20 foot lead as your dog gains confidence in transition areas.*

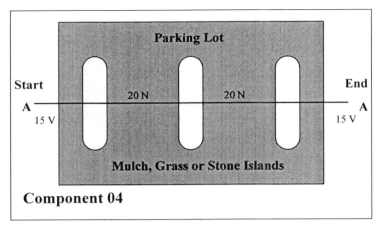

Component 04

(04) ACROSS ISLANDS

When your dog has mastered *Component 20*, this Component will increase the distance between the islands. Keep your dog working between the islands, not air scenting the track on the next island.

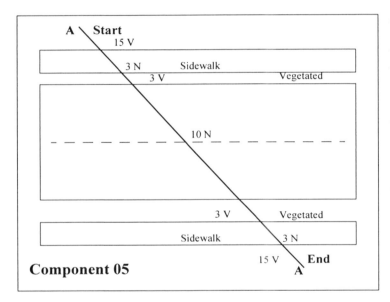

Component 05

(05) STREET CROSSINGS

This transition will require more training than most. Discrepancies in street construction both in the surfaces of the street and whether the street has curbs or not can effect the manner in which your dog tracks across the surface.

Curbs and Gutters as components are covered in a later chapter and are further discussed in the chapter regarding *Turn Components*. In the example above, you have multiple transitions on a single leg.

The track starts on a vegetated surface and crosses a sidewalk of some type of non-vegetated surface. From there you cross another vegetated area before reaching the street. If the street has gutters, you must train your dog to search in both directions at the curb *before* crossing the street. Once across the street, your dog will navigate a vegetated area, cross another sidewalk of some type of non-vegetated surface and then return to the vegetated area to continue the leg.

Your dog must become proficient in successfully following the track through many similar transition areas before you are ready to enter a test.

⌘ **Hint:** Spend time before practice sessions determining exactly what you will be attempting and your goals for the day. After the session, allocate additional time to discuss each track and the different opinion of how both the dog and handler performed during the exercise.

Chapter 18

Start Components

The **Start Components** of VST training are very important. Due to the inherent design of most urban locations where you will be training and where the vast majority of all VST tests will be held, VST starts are actually much harder than the starts you will train for in TD or TDX work.

As the start and at least the first fifteen yards of any test will be on a vegetated surface, you need to realize that these locations will be filled and surrounded by *scent obstacles* which your dog will need to work out before you progress into the non-vegetated parts of your track.

These *scent obstacles* may include some or all of the various combinations which we will work through in this chapter. They can include sidewalks, roads, parking lots, hedges, trees, buildings or a combination of all of these items.

To work your dog through each of these examples, take the *start component* and attempt to overlay it to your training area. Drive around your training site and look for locations containing these types of obstacles and distractions where you can plot similar components.

You will be modifying the components themselves to fit your training location in terms of length of legs or types of scent obstacles. Remember to train with each of these components in varying wind conditions and wind directions.

PHOTO BY SUE ANN THOMPSON

Start Components

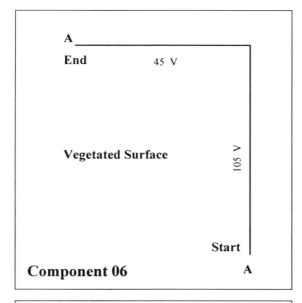

Component 06

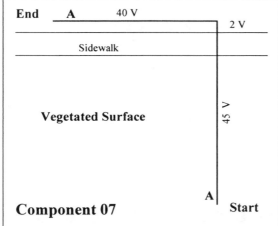

Component 07

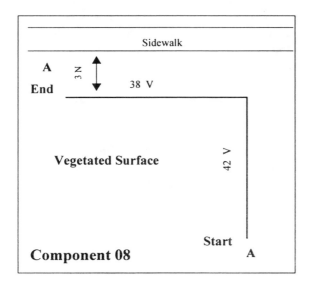

Component 08

(06) GRASS "L"

The most common of all starts for VST. Although this start seems simple, remember that most of the dogs entering a VST test fail on the non-vegetated areas or at the start.

Do not disregard this component. You will find that occasionally laying a series of all vegetated starts will keep your dog highly motivated and wanting to continue tracking.

(07) CROSSING A SIDEWALK

Crossing sidewalks, whether gravel, stone, dirt, concrete or asphalt, with an immediate turn is a difficult process for even dogs which have advanced in their VST training.

We have found that many dogs when introduced to this component (a) turn at or on the sidewalk and do not even attempt to search for a continuation of the track on the other side of the sidewalk *or* (b) jump the sidewalk without checking to see if the track possibly turned there.

(08) AVOIDING A SIDEWALK

Similar in difficulty to *Component 2* (Crossing a Sidewalk) this component tends to make you and your dog both think.

Imagine that you left the start and have covered the first 15 yards or so of vegetated surface. Now, in the back of your mind you expect the track to transition to non-vegetated surface. Immediately in front of you is a nice sidewalk; do you, believe your dog when he tells you there is a turn on the vegetated surface before the sidewalk; or do you attempt to push him to the sidewalk?

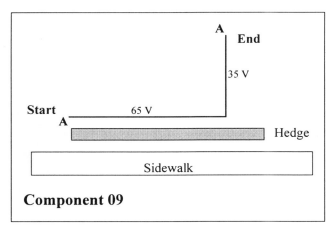

Component 09

(09) PARALLELING A HEDGE

Hedges, like walls or buildings will collect blown scent in the foliage and depending on wind direction may tend to make your dog follow the hedge line and not the original track.

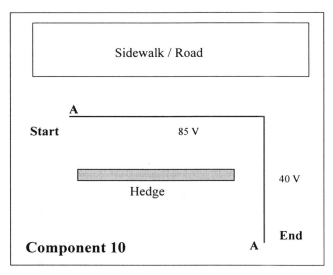

Component 10

(10) BETWEEN A HEDGE AND A SIDEWALK/ROAD

Similar in difficulty to Component 4, this component adds the additional dimension of a sidewalk or road for both pedestrian and vehicular distractions and depending upon current wind conditions, an opportunity for the scent to collect in another area.

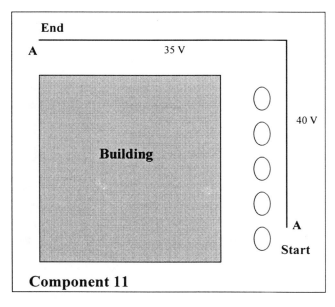

Component 11

(11) TREE LINE NEXT TO A BUILDING

Wind direction in this component is critical to your dog remaining on the track. If the wind is blowing over the building (left to right) it will tend to push the dog right of the track. Should the wind be blowing from right to left, it will tend to push your dog into the trees or even up against the building.

Lay this track in varying configurations as shown, next to the tree line and between the tree line and the building and practice in different wind conditions to teach your dog to follow the original track.

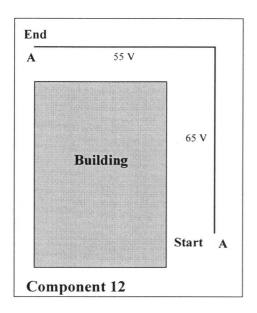

Component 12

(12) NEXT TO A BUILDING

As in *Component 6*, wind direction in this example will tend to push your dog off of the track.

The building effect or building shadow, as discussed in a previous chapter, can pull the dog towards the building.

Again practice in different wind conditions and distances from the building to teach your dog to follow the original track.

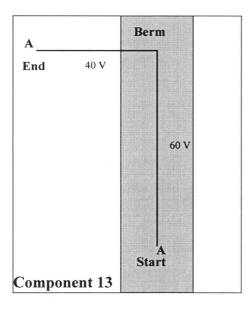

Component 13

(13) ON A BERM (Open Area)

Berms, small hills or the edges of dry retention ponds are likely locations for a start in a VST test.

The difference in elevation from the top of the berm to the normal ground level surrounding it will cause the scent to drift to the sides of the berm and down to the lower levels of the ground.

⌘ **Hint:** *When working this or any component involving scent obstacles with your dog, work at keeping your dog within the scent cone (approximately 3 feet on either side of the track). If your dog leaves the track to investigate an area, stand your ground, play out line, and wait for the dog to return to the track.*

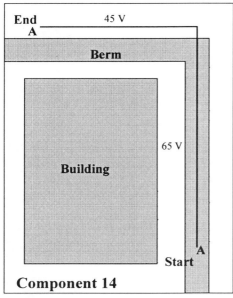

Component 14

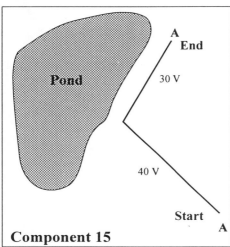

Component 15

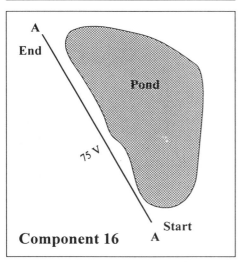

Component 16

(14) ON A BERM (Next To A Building)

Wind conditions in this example are more of a factor than those of *Component 8*.

The addition of the building shadow, swirling winds around the building compounded with the different elevations of the ground tends to pull the dog closer to the building and farther away from the track.

Practice by laying this track to the left, right, and on the berm and watch for differences in track indication by your dog on each of the track locations.

(15) TOWARDS A LAKE/POND

When working with starts or legs which go towards a lake, pond, or standing water, most dogs have the tendency to track through the turn and follow the drifting scent to the water's edge.

If your dog acknowledges or indicates the turn, stand your ground, and allow him enough lead to search beyond the turn. Don't move until he recommits to the track and the new leg.

(16) ALONG A LAKE/POND

As in *Component 10*, this type of start will tend to lead the dog off-track where he will attempt to follow the drifting scent along the contour of the lake or pond.

This is an excellent component to utilize to keep your dog on or within the scent cone. Plot practice tracks at varying distances from the water to see the direct influence the scent drifting to the water may have on your dog.

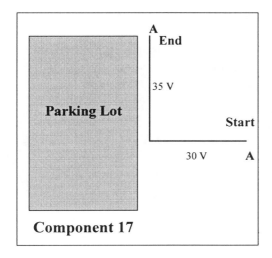

Component 17

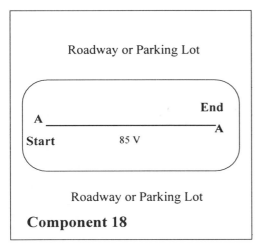

Component 18

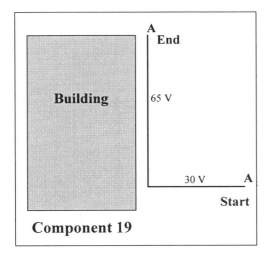

Component 19

(17) TOWARDS A PARKING LOT

Similar to *Component 3*, this component tends to make the handler attempt to push the dog through the turn and into the parking lot.

Train for this component. It is incorporated in most tests in one fashion or another. Allow your dog to work out the turn, even if he ventures into the parking lot.

(18) ON AN ISLAND

Although we have not actually seen this used as a start, we train for this to introduce the dogs to additional distractions of automobile and pedestrian traffic.

Depending on the actual site for your test, you may find such a component used as a leg after crossing a section of non-vegetated surface.

(19) TOWARDS A BUILDING

Unlike many other components which involve facing scent obstacles, this component is directly affected by wind and wind direction.

A crosswind (top to bottom or bottom to top) will push the scent along the building edge and lead the dog off track.

Wind blowing from the start (downwind) pushes the scent through the turn and into the edge of the building, while a wind blowing over the building (upwind) will tend to disperse the scent away from the building. This is an excellent component to intergrade into your training tracks to assist your dog in working in various wind conditions.

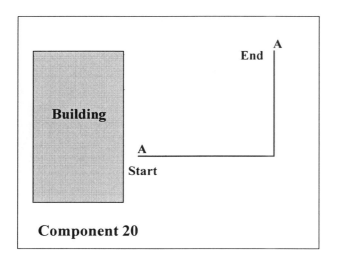

Component 20

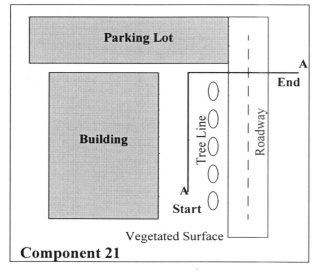

Component 21

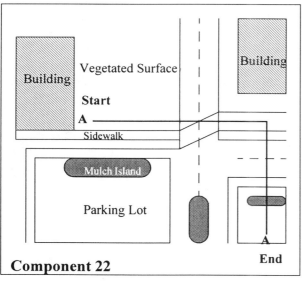

Component 22

(20) AWAY FROM A BUILDING

A start near a building or within the *building shadow* may cause some difficulty for your dog in determining the direction of the start leg.

Complicated Starts

The following two examples represent combinations of some of the previous *Components* to show some of the possibilities you may face at an actual test.

The inclusion of multiple components, buildings, roadways and sidewalks is what you should expect to see at your test.

Your individual track will differ from these examples, however, if you and your dog have progressed through the *Start Components*, you should have no apprehension as you approach the start flag of a test.

(21) A start between a building and a tree line with a turn before reaching a parking lot. The natural tendency of any handler will be to push the dog out into the parking lot. Watch the dog closely for turn indication, allow him to check out the parking lot if necessary, but remember the point of turn indication to allow you to get back to the track.

(22) A start leading away from a building and paralleling a sidewalk. The dog may work the indention at the edge of the sidewalk between the taller grass and the concrete surface. A quick transition to road surface, (asphalt), back to a concrete sidewalk, and a turn onto asphalt to reach a mulch island in an asphalt parking lot. One of the hardest starts we've seen and one we passed on!

Chapter 19

Turn Components

Turns shall be on various surfaces as dictated by the terrain. There shall be at least four (4) and not more than eight (8) turns on a track. Both right and left turns shall be used. At least three (3) of the turns shall be right angle (90 degree) turns and there should be more than three (3) such turns. Tracks may be laid along the sides of buildings and fences, through buildings with two or more openings or open sided, such as breezeways, shelters or roofed parking garages, but may not enter a building with closed doors and sides.

Prepare your dog for turns on both vegetated and non-vegetated surfaces. Working through these components will give you a better idea of what you may face in a test.

At least one (1) 90 degree turn shall be in an area devoid of vegetation and plotted to allow at least thirty (30) yards before crossing or returning to a vegetated surface. Acute angle turns are to be avoided.

*Judges shall not use the 90 degree non-vegetated turn in such a way as to be influenced by vegetation, but in fact said turn shall be a true **moment of truth** non-vegetated turn.*

When working on non-vegetated turns, do not expect your dog to indicate the turn in the same manner he indicates turns on vegetated surfaces. We have seen dogs slightly lift their heads, turn their head in the direction of the new leg or stop or start wagging their tail, but rarely have we seen dogs who will actively search for a non-vegetated turn without months of practice.

PHOTO BY CHRISTY BERGEON

Turn Components

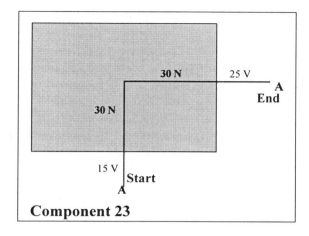

Component 23

(23) WINCHESTER

The **Moment Of Truth**. This turn is a requirement of the regulations - "*At least one 90 degree turn shall be in an area devoid of vegetation and plotted to allow at least thirty (30) yards before a change in surface.*"

Although believed by many that this turn must occur in a parking lot, the **Moment of Truth** may occur on other non-vegetated surfaces. Be prepared to see this turn or one similar to it at least once during your trip around your test track. If your dog can specialize on one component, this is the one to work toward. There is nothing that can describe the sight of a dog making a sharp 90 degree turn in a parking lot.

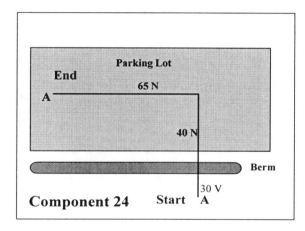

Component 24

(24) BERM AND WINCHESTER

This is a modified version of the standard Winchester turn with the addition of one or more berms. We have seen this combination used in more than one test.

Watch for wind direction and scent drifting when crossing the berm so that your dog remains lined up with the track when it reaches the non-vegetated surface. Allow the dog to work the transition area until it is confident in the track direction into the non-vegetated area.

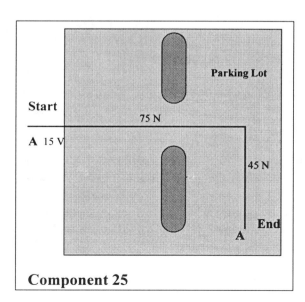

Component 25

(25) BETWEEN THE ISLANDS

When working in parking lots with islands, watch for scent drifting to the islands. If your dog insists on leaving the track to investigate the curbs or transition areas surrounding the islands, attempt to stand your ground and wait for the dog to return to the track.

If you must leave your position on the track to follow the dog while it discriminates between the blown or drifted scent and the actual track, remember to utilize the training hints covered earlier regarding *handler positioning.*

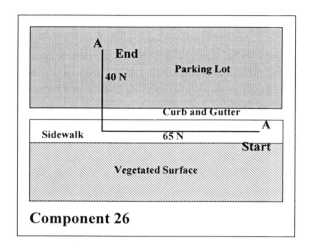

Component 26

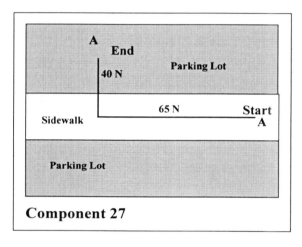

Component 27

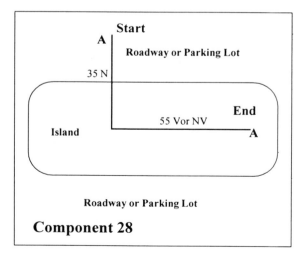

Component 28

(26) FROM/TO A SIDEWALK

Another difficult non-vegetated transition area occurs when you are turning off a sidewalk into a parking lot where the sidewalk is bordered on one side by a vegetated surface, and the other side by a curb and gutter. The first tendency of the dog is to work the curb area and not commit to the track on the pavement, or jump the sidewalk to work the scent on the vegetated surface.

Work slowly in these areas, allowing the dog to investigate the drifting scent, however, return your dog to the track if he has any difficulty.

(27) FROM/TO A SIDEWALK

In some non-vegetated areas such as large parking lots, you may find a wide sidewalk or pedestrian walkway. If the area is level with the parking surface, the only transition may be a simple change of surface texture.

However, if the sidewalk is elevated above the parking area, watch for scent drifting along the elevated edge between the sidewalk and the parking area.

(28) FROM/TO A ISLAND

Turns onto and off of islands require additional time to allow the dog to investigate the varying elevations and change of surface.

Many dogs seem to have problems remaining on the track when stepping off the island. The tendency is for them to check the curb or elevated surface at the point where the track changes elevation in the same manner as they would check with any curb and gutter component.

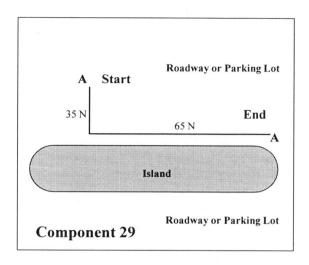

Component 29

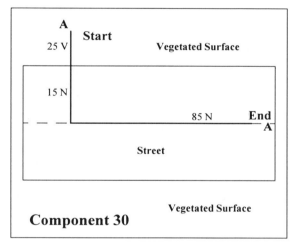

Component 30

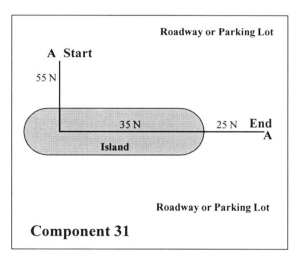

Component 31

(29) AVOIDING AN ISLAND

Scent collects along the edge of the island. In a turn immediately before the island, you can expect to find your dog working the curb of the island and perhaps the island itself before returning to the track. In turns away from the island, your dog will have a tendency to follow the scent down the edge of the island overshooting the turn. Allow your dog to work out these problems without working more than a lead length off of the track.

(30) TURNING ONTO A ROAD

A turn onto a road is one of the harder components to master. Your dog must be proficient with progressing through transition areas before working on this component. Remember that the painted lines, expansion joints and the point where two types of non-vegetated surfaces meet will hold scent and may lead your dog off track or cause it to parallel the track. Training in an area where you can somewhat control the scent drift by using the painted lines of the street to mark your turn will help your dog navigate this component.

(31) TURNING ONTO AN ISLAND

When working on a turn onto an island, remember that the scent will collect along the front edge of the island. In any wind condition, the scent may drift the entire length of the island causing your dog to attempt to parallel the track and not cross the island to reach the turn itself.

Training for this component on a grass island, before working on stone or mulch will allow your dog to build its confidence as it progresses.

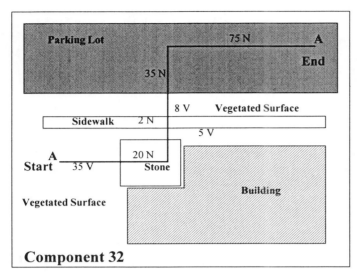

Component 32

MULTIPLE COMPONENT TURNS

(32) CHANGE OF SURFACES

In this example, the track starts on a vegetated surfaces, transitions to stone with a 90 degree turn; crosses a lawn, a concrete sidewalk, another strip of lawn and enters an asphalt parking lot to another 90 degree turn and long legs on asphalt. This example includes five transition areas, four types of surfaces and two 90 degree turns. The entire track is contained within the "*building shadow*" which will pull or push the scent and in windy conditions will cause the scent to swirl.

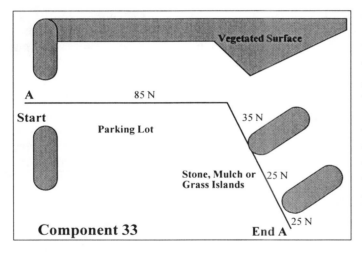

Component 33

End A

(33) ALONG THE ISLANDS

This example starts in a parking lot and contains an open turn followed by a leg which parallels the end of several islands. The start leg was a continuation of a leg in another parking lot. The open turn is unusual, as the handler would be expecting to find either a continuation of the leg past the island or a 90 degree turn before the islands. The islands will collect the tracklayers scent and may pull the dog onto the islands to confirm the track direction.

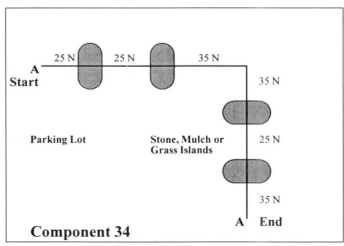

Component 34

(34) ACROSS THE ISLANDS

This example again starts in a parking lot, crosses two islands, makes a 90 degree turn and crosses two more islands. Treat this example as a series of multiple transition areas, allowing the dog to search around the curbs of the islands as it determine the track direction across the islands. This is an excellent motivational component for most dogs when used with or without the 90 degree turn.

Chapter 20

Building Components

PHOTO BY CHRISTY BERGEON

Tracks shall be laid utilizing any and all structures located on site and the diverse scenting conditions provided by such structures, such as buildings, fences, breezeways, ramps, stairs, bridges, shelters, roofed parking garages, through courtyards and buildings with two or more openings and/or open sided buildings. The intent of Variable Surface Tracking stresses that dogs shall be able to handle the diffusion of scent created by these structures. Tracks shall be as equal in complexity as possible in this regard. Judges shall not avoid plotting tracks in close proximity to buildings when they are available, it is feasible to do so and it will ensure a track that meets the intent of Variable Surface Tracking. Judges shall not plot tracks utilizing only one small shed type building or single fence line when the above options are available to plot fair but challenging tracks.

In variable surface tracking you **must** train for buildings. As the regulations state and the intent of VST is to work the dogs in an *urban* environment, your training around buildings will be one of the foundations your dog will require in order to pass the VST test. Buildings themselves offer a diverse and sometimes frustrating challenge to both the handler and the dog. Wind conditions, temperature and the distance from a building can all play major parts in your training and success around buildings. When working around buildings it is important to remember that you will be working in the *building shadow* which may effect the manner in which your dog remains on the track.

Many buildings are placed on built up areas of ground with slight to steep drop-off around the building causing the scent to roll down-hill and away from the track itself. Some are built with one or more landscaped berms around the buildings which can diffuse the scent. Trees, bushes, flower beds and hedges each will collect scent. The doors, walks, entrance ways, ramps and stairs around buildings will cause your dog to check out these crevices and collection areas.

Your job as a handler is to work your dog sufficiently around these distractions to allow him to remain on the track. In order to do that, you will need to practice these components at varying distances from the buildings. Your dog may react differently if the component is plotted at 18 inches from a building than it will when it is plotted 5 yards from a building. In an effort to help our dogs understand what scent can do around buildings, we plot these components at 18 inches, 2 yards, 5 yards, 10 yards and 15 yards from the building.

Building Components

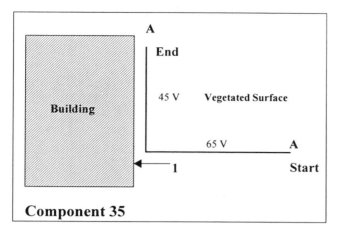

Component 35

(Building, End, 45 V Vegetated Surface, 65 V, A, 1, Start)

(35) INTO THE BUILDING

A leg which has been plotted towards a building [1] will tend to pull the dog to the building even if the turn has been plotted 3, 5 or even 10 yards from the building.

As you work with your dog, look for any slight indication that he has found the turn, even if he continues to be drawn into the building. Many dogs have failed in VST by being pulled into the building and walking past an article laid only a few yards away on the actual track.

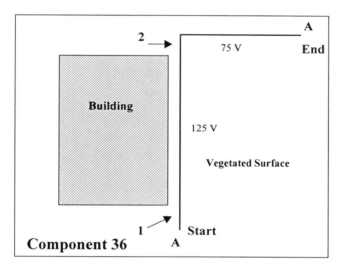

Component 36

(Building, 2, 75 V, End, 125 V, Vegetated Surface, 1, Start, A)

(36) PAST THE BUILDING

When tracks are plotted in this manner, the dog will tend to search at the first corner of the building [1] for the track. it may appear as if the track has turned at this point due to swirling winds around the building. As the dog works through this problem, he is then faced with a similar problem at the other end of the building [2].

At point [1], stand your ground and allow the dog to determine for himself that the track continues on. When you reach point [2], the dog may attempt to turn the corner, following swirling scent around the building. Again stand your ground and allow the dog to search, gently assisting if necessary to keep him on the track.

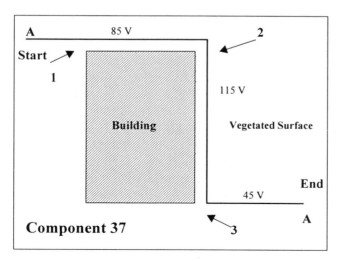

Component 37

(A, 85 V, 2, Start, 1, 115 V, Building, Vegetated Surface, End, 45 V, A, 3)

(37) AROUND THE BUILDING

As in *Component 35* your dog may have problems at areas [1], [2] and [3]. The buildings tend to pull the dogs around the corners and the dog must work these areas often enough to become confident with staying on the track.

You can assist your dog in these exercises by standing your ground, releasing enough lead for the dog to check and discard the blown or swirling scent and then allow the dog to return to the original track.

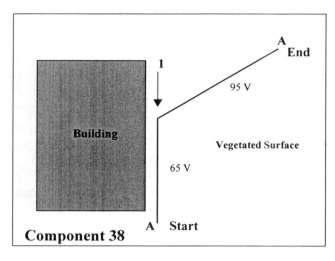

Component 38

(38) INTO AND AWAY FROM THE BUILDING

An open turn away from a building may be one of the more difficult building components for you and your dog to master. In most cases, due to blown or swirling scent, the dog will continue down the leg, through the turn [1] for another 3-20 yards before it determines it has run out of the scent cone.

You must be prepared to help your dog as it searches for the turn by utilizing *handler positioning* and backing up to allow your dog to work back to and execute the turn properly.

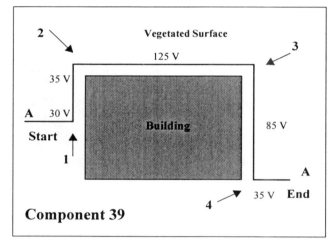

Component 39

(39) INTO AND AROUND THE BUILDING

This component is based on a leg towards the building, following the building shape and a turn away from the building at a corner.

The start and second leg [1] and [2] you have worked through in previous components and your dog should be confident in following the actual track. Turn 3 [3] follows the building and may cause your dog, depending on wind conditions, to attempt to track away from the building for a period of time. Turn 4 [4] again is away from the building at the corner and a potential change or shift in wind direction.

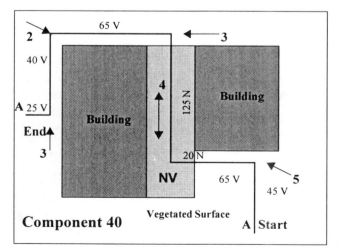

Component 40

(40) INTO, AROUND AND BETWEEN TWO BUILDINGS

As in the above components, wind direction and swirling scent combined with transitions to and from non-vegetated surfaces are the problem areas for most dogs. The entire leg [4] between the buildings, depending on wind direction is a problem leg for most dogs to stay on the track. The tendency is for them to work both edges of the buildings, casting across the track. Article placement on this leg (if any) is critical. In given conditions, it would be possible for the dog to work down only one building and therefore miss an article placed along the other building.

Chapter 21

Fence, Hedge and Wall Components

PHOTO BY CHRISTY BERGEON

Fence, Hedges and Walls

Tracks which are laid along or near fences tend to draw the dog away from the track and toward or along the fence. Various types of fencing material collect more or less scent and the scent collection may reflect on how close your dog will follow the track.

In the VST tracks used in our examples, the most common forms of fencing found in tests are:

• Link Fences (Chain Link And Plastic Snow Fences)

Depending on the distance from the track to the fence. These fences will draw in your dog like magnets. Between a building and a fence, at a distance of about 10 yards, your dog will either work the side of the building or parallel the base of the fence. The numerous links in these fences collect airborne scent and can create a wall of scent for your dog to follow.

In open areas, the airborne scent can move from the track and collect on the fence at distances of 20 or 30 yards. When working near fences of this type, work with your dog to stay on or near the original track and teach him to discriminate between the collected airborne scent on the fence and the original track.

•Wooden Fences (Horizontal Cross Rail - Horse Fences, Etc.)

Typically buiit using large fence posts and smaller horizontal cross rails. These fences tend to collect scent along the base of the vertical fence posts. The action and reaction of your dog working along such a fence line should allow you to determine whether he is actually on track or is "jumping" from scent pool to scent pool at the base of the fence posts.

◆**Wooden Fences (Vertical Slats)**

These fences tend to collect the scent as a masonry or brick wall would. The rough surface of the boards and the available surface area of the fence will draw your dog off track and to the fence.

◆ **Brick Or Masonry Fences And Walls**

Typically a rough surface whether stucco, brick, cinder-block, etc. These fences and walls pull, collect and hold the scent along their surface area and in the grout lines between the building components.

Fence Components

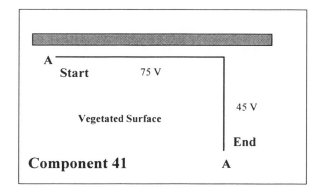

Component 41

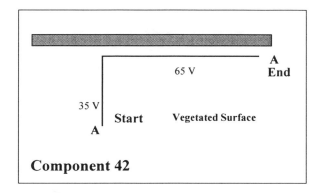

Component 42

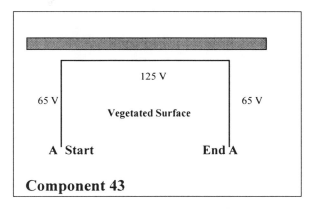

Component 43

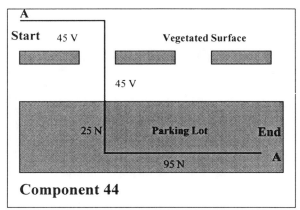

Component 44

(41) ALONG AND AWAY FROM A FENCE

Wind conditions and track placement in relation to the distance from the fence, hedge or wall will affect the performance of your dog.

(42) TOWARD AND ALONG A FENCE

When heading for a fence, hedge or wall, the make-up or structure of the fence and the distance of the turn and leg from it will determine the amount of pull the fence will have on this track.

Keeping you dog on-track will be one of your keys to success in VST on these types of components. These areas appear to be especially inviting to judges as a place to leave an article.

(43) TOWARD, ALONG AND AWAY FROM A FENCE

In TDX work this would be known as *obstacle denial*. Heading for an obstacle and then turning to parallel it and then again away from the obstacle. In VST, there are no physical obstacles to conquer so you can expect to see this type of component utilized in various implementations along the track.

(44) PARALLEL TO & BETWEEN A FENCE

VST tracks will go between fences, open gates or opening in walls or hedges in an effort to get to another portion of the track. In this component, the concern should not be in entering the opening, but the distance between the next turn and the fence. If the distance is too close, the dog may parallel the fence and not complete execute the proper turn, potentially missing an article.

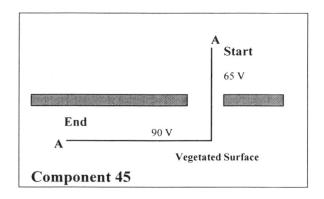

Component 45

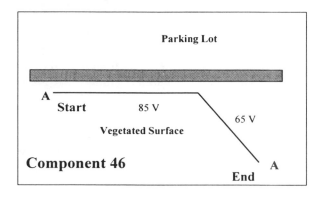

Component 46

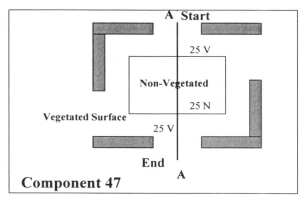

Component 47

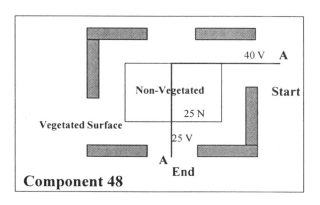

Component 48

(45) BETWEEN A FENCE

You can expect, depending on the site for your test, to see at least one portion of your track go through an opening, gate or between two fences to reach another portion of the track. In this component, the dog may stop on both sides of the opening to determine that the track did indeed pass through the opening. In windy conditions, the dog could be forced or drawn through the opening or the scent could be dispersed on one side of the opening confusing the dog in the direction of the track.

(46) OPEN TURN AWAY FROM A FENCE

A turn away from a fence, hedge or wall is another difficult problem solving situation for your dog. Wind conditions can push the scent farther down the fence causing your dog to overshoot the turn and cast or backtrack to locate the turn

(47) THROUGH A COURTYARD

Tracking through a multiple opening courtyard with swirling winds and blowing scent may cause your dog to work many of the interior surfaces of the courtyard and check out several potential exit locations before determining the exact direction of the track. Work these areas slowly and allow your dog to inspect the area within the length of the lead.

(48) TURN IN A COURTYARD

Another variation of the courtyard with the addition of a turn along a transition area. Remember that the scent will flow from the actual turn along any indentions or elevation changes in the transition area. Determining the exact location of the turn may be difficult under swirling wind conditions, however, by working slowly and calmly the dog should determine the turn and new track direction with experience.

Chapter 22

Curbs and Gutters Components

Scent can be blown into a gutter, confusing the dog

Curbs and Gutters

Curbs and gutters accumulate scent and the dogs will typically leave the actual track to follow the *fresher* or *stronger* scent along the curb or in the indention caused by the gutter. Your dog will often parallel the actual track, sometimes by as much as 10-20 yards.

In many cases, dogs which have been trained in TDX work have been conditioned to cross or "jump" roads. While in VST, you will be expected to cross, turn next to, turn down or parallel a roadway, sidewalk or non-vegetated surface which may have a curb or gutter along one or both sides of the surface. It is important for you dog to learn to search for the actual scent of the tracklayer (footsteps) when it encounters a roadway.

When introducing your dog to these areas, allow the dog to search the curb or gutter to motivate him to return to the actual track.

Working a curb at the edge of a parking lot

Curbs and Gutters Components

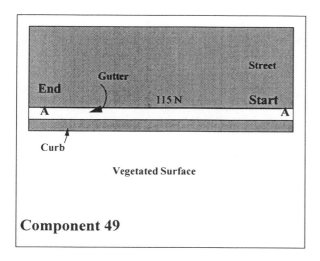

Component 49

(49) ALONG THE GUTTER

Tracking parallel to a curb or gutter will introduce you to several new scenting problems. If the track is laid parallel to the gutter, the scent will collect in the lowest area, along the intersection of the curb and gutter, and may pull your dog off track.

This component is an excellent training method for introducing your dog to long legs of non-vegetated surfaces. Tracking along the gutter itself, due to the collection of scent, appears to be very easy for most dogs. You need to watch very carefully the indications or distractions which can be caused by the scent being drawn into storm drains along the gutter.

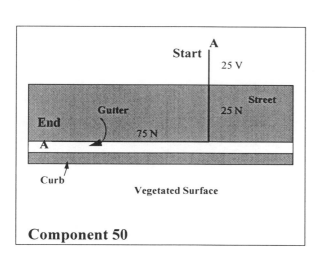

Component 50

(50) TURNS INTO GUTTERS FROM NON-VEGETATED SURFACES

When crossing a street and turning into a gutter, the natural tendency of the dog will to be to cross the gutter and search for the track on the vegetated surface.

Stand your ground and allow the dog to search for the track to the end of the lead. Do not move until the dog has committed to the track in the gutter, then praise him. If he is having difficulty, move up the line to a position of about six feet from the dog and assist him in locating the track in the gutter.

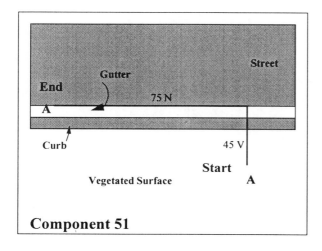

Component 51

(51) TURNS INTO GUTTERS FROM VEGETATED SURFACES

When turning into a gutter from a vegetated surface, the dog will normally overshoot the turn and search in or jump the street. Stand your ground and move up the lead if necessary to assist the dog in determining the track.

In each of these *Components*, the scent will flow in both directions along the gutter and your dog will need to learn to problem solve the actual direction of the track.

Chapter 23

Elevation Components

PHOTO BY ED PRESNALL

When working around buildings, in addition to flat lawns and flowerbeds, we have found three basic landscaping formats which change the elevation around the buildings.

■ STAIRSTEP LANDSCAPING
The ground is terraced away from the building. Each terrace may be made up of mulch beds, railroad ties, bricks or other substances and may be from three to ten yards wide. The scent will collect on the varying elevations, along plants, hedges or flower beds and may tend to cause your dog to work in an erratic manner.

■ BERM LANDSCAPING
A berm is placed around the building or around a particular side of a building to assist in drainage or for esthetic appearances. These berms seem to be a natural magnet for judges to plot tracks on. The scent will roll down on both sides of the building and may collect up next to the building.

■ DROP-OFF LANDSCAPING
The ground is graded in a manner to cause a drop-off away from the building. The scent tends to spread down the drop-off and away from the original track.

It is important to remember that scent will flow in a downhill manner, collecting at elevation points, changes in cover, landscaping material or along plants and allow your dog to inspect and reject multiple areas while determining the location and direction of the track.

In each of these *Elevation Components*, we have establish three likely positions of the track for you to work with. Remember that each of these locations is within the *building shadow* and the building itself may pull or push the scent away from the track.

Elevation Components

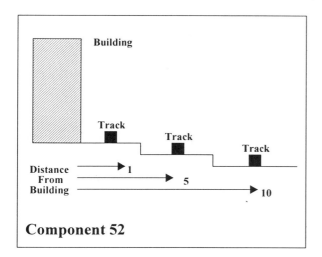

Component 52

(52) STAIRSTEP LANDSCAPING

When working in stairsteped locations in close proximity to a building, portions of the scent may be pulled toward the building while some of the blown or drifting scent will flow downhill to the next lower elevation.

Work slowly with your dog to stay on the track. We have found that when working in these locations, the utilization of several articles on a long leg will help maintain your dogs motivation and enthusiasm.

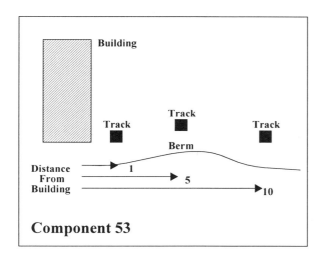

Component 53

(53) BERM LANDSCAPING

Berms near buildings create scenting problems which have caused the failure of many dog to remain on the track. The scent will flow down both sides of the berm and amy be drawn to the building, leading your dog off track and away from an article.

When starting your dog in these areas, work closely, 6-10 feet from the dog, allowing him to search, but remaining well within the scent cone.

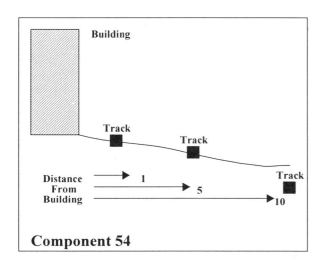

Component 54

(54) DROP-OFF LANDSCAPING

In this type of elevation locations, it is normal for the dog to work downhill from the actual track.

Placing random articles along the track will allow your dog to follow closer to the track. As your dogs proficiency and confidence increases in these areas, reduce the number of articles.

Chapter 24

Alleys and Walkways Components

It will be the rare test when you do not see a portion of the track run behind or between buildings through alleyways or along walks, courtyards or non-vegetated recreational areas.

Prepare your dog for these situations by training with the following components. Remember that you are working within the building shadow of the surrounding structures and wind may swirl between the buildings creating a tunnel effect which could confuse your dog, as to the track location, or push your dog along past any turns or articles. These tunnels can cause your dog to overshoot corners or turn into blind alleyways or appear confused at doorways and stairs along the track.

Work these areas slowly and on a short lead. Allow the dog to check out and disregard doorways, dumpsters, ledges and the like that you may find along the track and always encourage your dog to return to the track.

Tracking into a walled courtyard on brick pavers

Alleys and Walkways Components

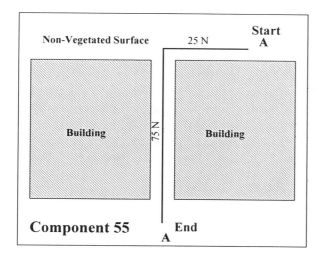

Component 55

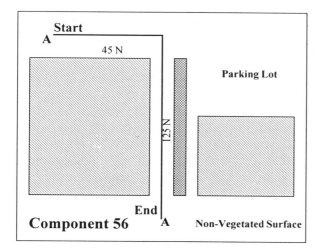

Component 56

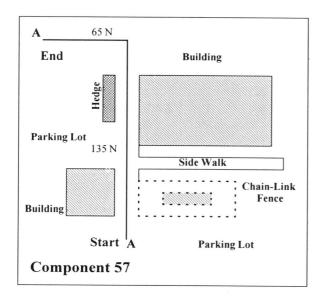

Component 57

(55) ALLEYWAY BETWEEN BUILDINGS

Even in light wind, a swirling and tunnel effect will be created by the close proximity of the buildings. As you work your dog towards the turn, depending upon on the wind direction, the dog may overshoot the turn and require a moment to determine the track direction.

As you work between the buildings, the wind may swirl and your dog may work leave the track to cast along either wall. Again, as you exit the alleyway, the dog may attempt to follow the blown scent along the side of the building before determining the track direction.

(56) BETWEEN A BUILDING AND A FENCE

Similar in difficulty to *Component 54*, this component adds additional variables based on the construction of the fence or wall. A solid wood or masonry wall will collect scent along the base of the wall, however the dog should learn to quickly differentiate between the blown scent in this situation and the track itself.

If the fence is a plastic or chain-link fence, the scent will collect along the length of the fence and tends to pull the dog off-track. Working closely to your dog will allow you better control while offering additional confidence to your dog.

(57) ALLEYS BETWEEN STRUCTURES

Alleyways and walkways can be created with structures, fences and hedges. Although each segment of the leg requires specific reinforcement, the entire leg is a complex scenting condition.

As the dog starts, it is faced with a track between a structure and a chain link enclosure. The dog may attempt to follow the chain link fencing due to the accumulation of blown scent. As the dog continues on, a tunnel is formed by the sidewalk and building. The hedge ahead, will pull the dog away from the track and as the dog passes the corner of the building and hedge may be faced with crosswinds pushing it in front of the building or forcing an early turn.

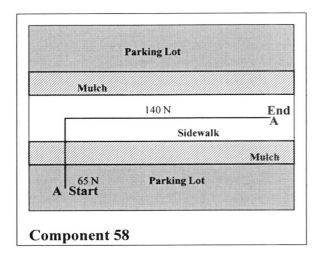

Component 58

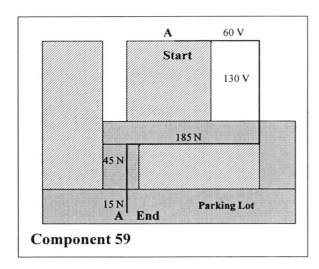

Component 59

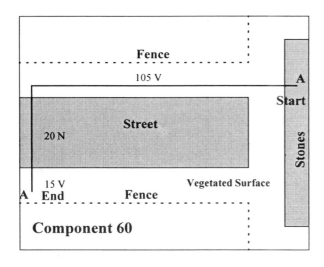

Component 60

(58) SIDE WALKS IN PARKING LOTS

Large sidewalks or walkways in parking lots have been utilized in several tests. In this example, the mulch beds and sidewalk are raised approximately six inches above the parking lot. The change in elevation, curbs and change in surfaces all create a situation which is likely to confuse the dog.

Allow the dog to work the elevation change at the curb slowly and assist him as required to find and execute the turn. Many dogs will attempt to jump the sidewalk until their proficiency on non-vegetated surfaces has increased to a point where they actively search for changes in direction and surface textures.

(59) WALKWAYS BETWEEN BUILDINGS

A vegetated leg with a transition to non-vegetated surfaces combined with a turn at the edge of a building is a very difficult component for most dogs to accomplish. The tendency, normally due to wind currents and blown scent, is for the dog to overshoot the turn and continue down the building, cutting off several legs and perhaps missing an article.

Work slowly in any transition area. Once the dog has executed the turn, a tunnel effect may pull or push the dog off track. When training in such areas, work closely to your dog.

(60) PARALLELING STREETS AND FENCES

An alleyway can be created between the fences, even though the distance between them is approximately 50 yards wide. The fences may pull the dog off track, while the street, if it has curbs and gutters may draw the dog.

Be watchful of wind currents which might push the dog down the track and through the turn or may keep the dog working one of the fence lines. Due to the width of this area, work the dog with about 10 feet of lead, giving additional lead as necessary to allow the dog to inspect and reject pooling scent.

Chapter 25

Standing Water Components

PHOTO BY ED PRESNALL

Standing Water

When working on variable surfaces you may be faced with tracking through standing water. The water may have collected in pools from low spots in parking lots, along curbs and gutters after or during a rain, or from run-off from automatic sprinkler systems.

The scent will flow with the water, spreading out from the track and collecting along the edges of the collection area. As your dog tracks up to one of these areas, he may indicate loss of scent and search the edges of the area, following the scent in an erratic pattern along the water's edge.

Allow your dog to search these areas, watching for any indications he may give you as to the direction of the track. Corners laid in or near these areas are extremely distracting to the dogs and will require extreme patience by the handler to work through these areas.

In working in areas such as business parks and campuses with automatic watering systems, it will not be unusual for you to lay a track across a dry area of non-vegetated surface, only to return several hours later to find that all or portions of the area have been covered with standing water.

Working through the following components will prepare you for such situations on test day.

Standing Water Components

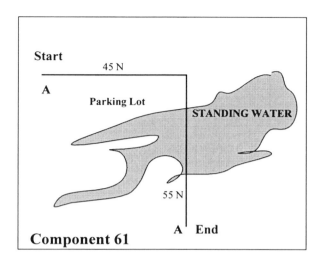

Component 61

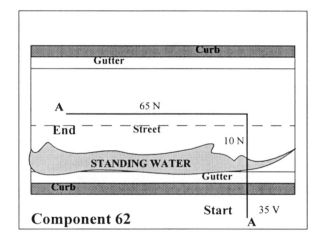

Component 62

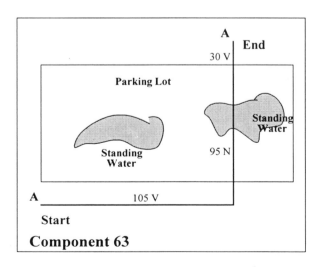

Component 63

(61) WATER FLOW FROM SPRINKLERS

At some point in your training you will encounter standing or flowing water across your track. Normally this is runoff from the sprinkler system on the surrounding vegetated surfaces. We search for these areas and time the sprinkler systems to allow us to plot the track when it is dry and run it after the sprinklers have operated and the runoff is on the track.

The dog will work the edges of the water flow, slowly being pulled off the track. Practice of this component will prepare you for the day when you encounter this situation in a test, while enhancing your dogs problem solving abilities.

(62) WATER ALONG GUTTERS

Rain or runoff from sprinkler systems will collect in the gutters of a street. Even when the runoff has dissipated, the damp surface will draw scent and pull the dog off-track.

This component will introduce your dog to damp or wet scenting conditions on non-vegetated surfaces. If you are working on this component in a dry climate or during a dry period in your area, carry a one or two gallon bucket of water with you and dump the water into the gutter as you lay the track. When you return to run the track, the surface will still be damp and will be collecting scent from the track.

(63) WATER IN LOW SPOTS

In some parking lots or non-vegetated areas, there are low spots which collect runoff or rain water. Tracking through these areas creates a similar situation as defined in *Component 61* and runoff from sprinkler systems. The variable in this component is that the water is normally not flowing and may be stagnant.

Scenting in these situations is difficult for the dogs, however introduction to and experience with this situation will allow your dog to problem solve and work through the situation.

Chapter 26

Stairs and Ramps Components

On may tracks you may find stairs or ramps which your dog may be required to navigate. Although not technically an obstacle in VST work, these items require training to allow your dog to become comfortable when working on them.

If you have a dog which tracks very fast, you must slow the dog down in order to safely navigate these parts of a track. You and your dogs safety should be of utmost concern.

There are three basic types of stairs which you may encounter in your training. The long, low landscaping type steps which front many buildings should bot be a problem to master. The *Elevation Components* should prepare you to handle these types of steps.

The long risers, normally found leading up to the front doors of buildings or as stairway to a floor below ground level or within a parking garage are usually manufactured with a back panel which forms a solid stair. The scent will collect on each level, however the closed back manufacturing technique reduces the amount of blown scent.

The difficult stairs to master for both you and your dog appear to be open risers or floating steps which are made without a back panel. These types of stairs allow the scent to blow around and through the staircase and can confuse your dog when approaching or working near them.

Ramps such as found in a loading dock area or everyday wheelchair ramps are normally manufactured with a brushed finish to the concrete which holds scent. Most dogs do not have a problem with becoming acclimated to working on ramps and with training can become very accomplished at following the scent up and down ramps.

Stairs and Ramps Components

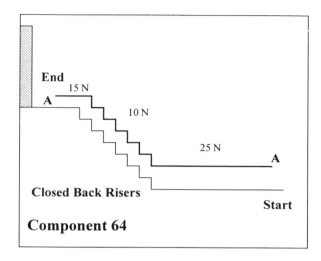

Closed Back Risers

Component 64

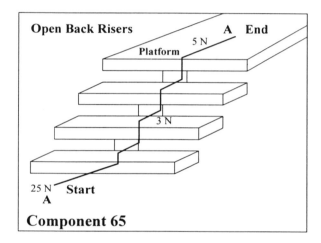

Open Back Risers

Component 65

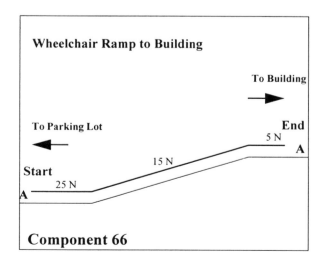

Wheelchair Ramp to Building

Component 66

(64) CLOSED BACK RISERS

In most locations you will find *closed back riser* stairs normally made from bricks, masonry or concrete. In some cases the stairs may only be 3 or 4 risers and in other as many as 25 or more. Train with your dog in working up and down these areas.

As you progress in your training, add turns at the top or bottom of the stairs to simulate actual test situations. For safety reasons, do not allow your dog to run or pull you up or down the stairs. Allow your dog enough lead to commit to the stairs and work them slowly. Remember that the scent will pool near the back of each riser and will spread out along the stair depending upon wind conditions.

(65) OPEN BACK RISERS

In many campus locations you will find *open back riser* stairs. These are much more difficult for your dog to navigate due to the spreading and blowing of scent through and around the risers. The scent may fall through the risers and pool under the stairs causing some confusion in your dog committing to the direction of the track.

Do not allow your dog to run or pull you up or down the stairs. Give your dog enough lead to commit to the stairs and work them slowly.

(66) WHEELCHAIR RAMPS

Most buildings have wheel chair access ramps as well as stairs. The surface of these ramps is usually in a brushed or ribbed concrete to allow for better traction in inclement weather. The scent will adhere to this surface and most dogs do not have difficulty in working ramps.

Be prepared to meet pedestrian traffic both going in your direction and coming towards you and your dog. If in a training or test situation you are working on a ramp and meet someone in a wheel chair coming towards you, remember that the ramp was developed for them and you are intruding upon their space.

Chapter 27

Open Buildings and Garages Components

PHOTO BY ED PRESNALL

Open Structures and Garages

The Regulations state *Tracks may be laid along the sides of buildings and fences, through buildings with two or more openings or open sided, such as breezeways, shelters or roofed parking garages, but may not enter a building with closed doors and sides.*

As you work with your dog, remember to train your dog inside and around parking garages and work the dog through open sided buildings, shelters and breezeways. The scenting conditions *in* or *near* these structures may be harder for your dog to discriminate due to the swirling wind through the structures openings.

When working in these areas, keep your dog on track while changing direction and discriminating between the actual track and blown scent. Such blown scent may cling to surfaces and walls or may be blown out of the structure through the openings.

When tracking in parking garages, always watch for traffic and dangerous substances which may be on the surface.

PHOTO BY ED PRESNALL

Open Buildings and Garages Components

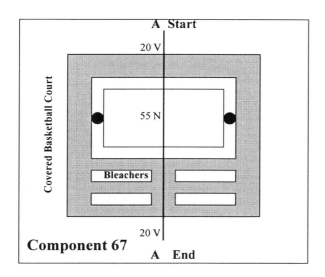

Component 67

(67) OPEN SIDED BUILDINGS

When working around open sided structures, the scent may swirl or drift and collect on elevated areas, around walls or support posts. In this example, when the dog nears the bleachers it may have difficulties determining the track and may want to search around or under the bleachers.

Continue to work slowly around any supports, walls, furnishings or changes in elevation within the open structure.

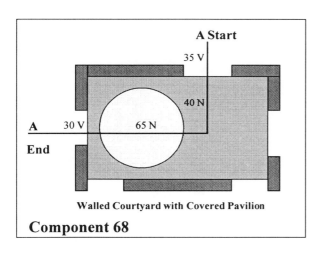

Walled Courtyard with Covered Pavilion
Component 68

(68) PAVILIONS

Adding an additional degree of difficulty to working around open structures is the partially enclosed courtyard surrounding this pavilion.

Depending on the wind conditions, the openings in the walls of the courtyard will cause the scent to swirl or may create a tunnel effect across the courtyard area.

Potential problems you may face in training for this component include multiple transitions, change of elevation between the courtyard and the pavilion and swirling or drifting scent.

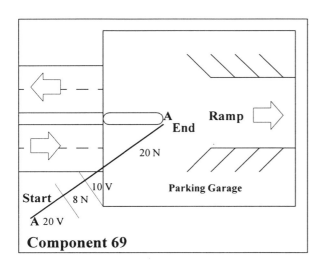

Component 69

(69) PARKING GARAGES

The polished surface of the floor combined with swirling or blowing wind creates numerous scent obstacles for your dog to overcome during training. When working in these areas, remain close to your dog, helping him to determine the track location and direction.

Be wary of loud noises which may echo off the walls, frightening your dog. If at all possible, appoint someone to watch for traffic.

Chapter 28

Automobile Components

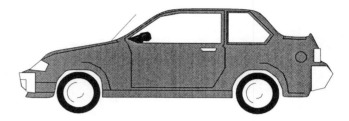

When working in parking lots and garages, you and your dog will come into contact with vehicles which are parked along or near your track or which may be moving across your track. As your track is laid, the scent will drift to and under the surrounding automobiles.

Vehicles which arrive and park along your track after it is laid tend to become appealing to most dogs. This could be due to the fact that they collect more scent due to the increased heat of the engine or the new smells of the vehicle are simply more appealing to the dog.

Practice these components around parked vehicles. In some training areas, you may be able to lay your track before all of the cars have arrived for the day to watch the reaction of your dog in these area.

Leaving the track to evaluate a recently parked vehicle

Automobile Components

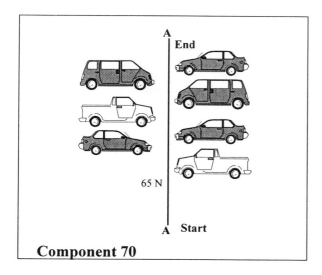

Component 70

(70) TRACK BETWEEN AUTOMOBILES

When your track runs between a line of cars, the dog will sometimes stop to sniff or check out the cars along the way. People or vehicles entering and exiting the track area will further contaminate the track area.

If curbs or bumpers separate the vehicles, the scent will collect along the elevated edge and help your dog remain on-track.

Due to the amount of pedestrian traffic in these areas most articles placed along the track in this area will be moved or removed.

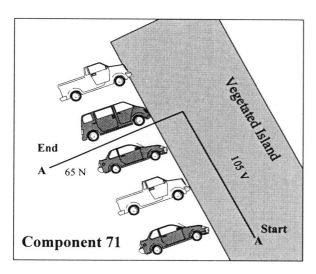

Component 71

(71) TURN OFF OF ISLAND BETWEEN AUTOMOBILES

The transition from vegetated to non-vegetated surfaces is further compounded by the people and vehicles entering and exiting the track area.

Once the dog determines the turn location, you may need to help the dog with the transition into the parking lot. Automobiles may have parked on the turn and you may need to help your dog work around parked cars in order to regain the track location.

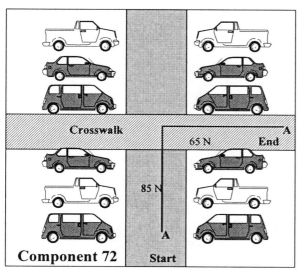

Component 72

(72) TURN ON CROSSWALK

Wind drift in the driveway area may spread the scent to the facing lines of automobiles. The turn area may be further contaminated with crosswalk traffic.

If your dog is having difficulty remaining on track, move up the line to offer additional support and confidence.

Watch carefully for vehicle or pedestrian traffic when training on this component.

Chapter 29

Component Tracks

Component Tracks

- ☐ Developed by implementing modified versions of individual components into your training area.

- ☐ Start with a site plan of your training area.

- ☐ Overlay individual components on the site plan to "*build*" a component track.

- ☐ Include several component types to create a complete track.

- ☐ Try to keep the complete track in a linear format with enough room between legs to compensate for wind direction or wind shift.

- ☐ Do not allow the tracks to loop back on themselves or set the dogs up for failure by creating situations where the dog can overshoot a corner and run into another leg of the track.

- ☐ Article placement is critical. Do not hide articles or place them in positions along the track where the dog can miss them by following the natural contours of the landscaping, drop-off or curb and gutter areas.

- ☐ When you have evaluated your training site completely, you will find that it is very easy to substitute components to vary the track layout. Attempt to build component tracks that are similar to or match specific areas of a site where you expect to enter a test.

- ☐ Train in all weather and wind conditions to be prepared for test day.

Component Tracks

COMPONENT TRACK	COMPONENT ENHANCEMENT	PAGE
◆ **01**	The Start Component could be modified to either turn before or on the sidewalk, offering a different training exercise. By modifying the leg lengths, this Component Track can offer multiple non-vegetated turns on gravel and stone. Additionally, you could extend the leg lengths to cross the berm in two positions or position the track between the berm and the building.	143
◆ **02**	The first turn could be modified to turn at the building and follow the building into the parking lot as Component 36. Due to the potential of scent blowing across the parking lot, we would not recommend turning in front of the top building. We would also not recommend attempting to go around the small lake at the top due to the possibility of the dog being pulled into the wall and cutting off the track. The end of the track could pass through the courtyard without turning, but should not turn towards the parking lot for the end.	144

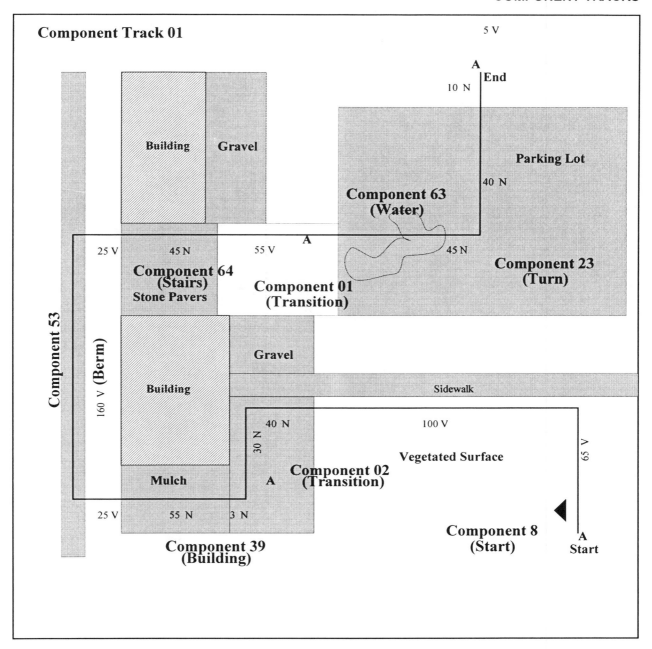

Component Track 01

5 V

A End

10 N

Building | Gravel

Parking Lot

40 N

Component 63 (Water)

25 V | 45 N | 55 V | A | 45 N

Component 64 (Stairs) Stone Pavers

Component 01 (Transition)

Component 23 (Turn)

Component 53

160 V (Berm)

Gravel

Building

Sidewalk

40 N

30 N

100 V

Vegetated Surface

65 V

Component 02 (Transition)

Mulch

A

Component 8 (Start)

25 V | 55 N | 3 N

A Start

Component 39 (Building)

COMPONENT	TYPE	PAGE	DESCRIPTION
Component 8	Start	93	Crossing A Sidewalk
Component 02	Transition	89	Across Dirt/Mulch/Gravel
Component 39	Building	108	Into and Around The Building
Component 53	Elevation	119	Berm Landscaping
Component 64	Stairs	131	Closed Back Risers
Component 01	Transition	89	Direct Transition
Component 63	Water	127	Water Flow From Sprinklers
Component 23	Turn	105	Winchester (The Moment of Truth)

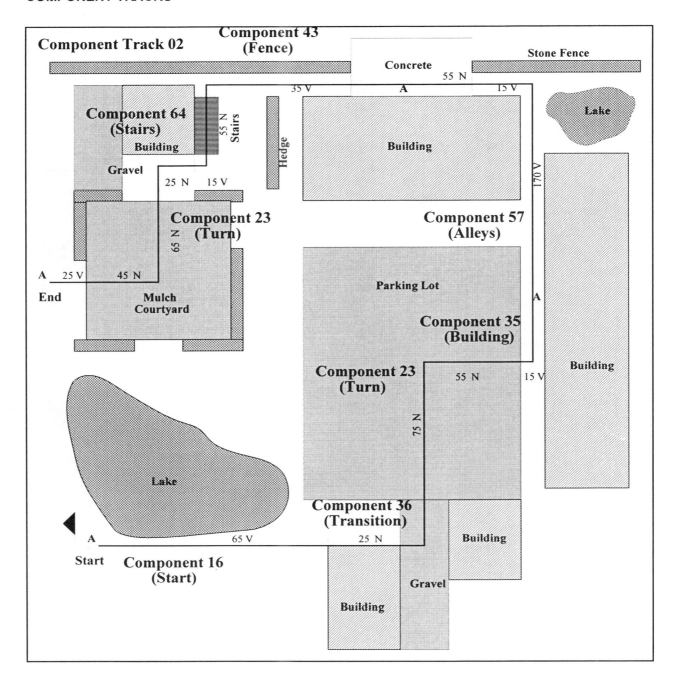

COMPONENT	TYPE	PAGE	DESCRIPTION
Component 16	Start	96	Along A Lake/Pond
Component 02	Transition	89	Across Dirt/Mulch/Gravel
Component 23	Turn	108	Winchester (The Moment of Truth)
Component 35	Building	35	Into The Building
Component 57	Alley	123	Alleys Between Structures
Component 43	Transition	111	Toward, Along and Away From A Fence
Component 64	Stairs	131	Closed Back Risers (Stairs)
Component 23	Turn	105	Winchester (The Moment of Truth)

Chapter 30

Test Preparation

Test Preparation

Before you complete that entry form and mail off your entry fee, think about the other components of the test which will have a direct effect on your performance.

☐ **Site**

If the test site is a government facility, business park or campus location, contact the administrator and request a copy of the architects site plan. The drawing will display all building placements, parking lots, common maintenance areas (islands, flower beds, parks, etc.), easements, garages and landscaping features of the site.

If at all possible, spend a day or two walking the site and plotting tracks as if you were the judges. If the facility allows, take your dog and plot and run actual tracks at the site.

Take the site plan and *overlay* it onto the site plan for your current training facilities. Are there similar building placements, landscaping features or garages? Go to your training sites and plot components which simulate tracking at the proposed test site. Be prepared. Do not assume that because tests have been held at this location before you will not have problems. Practice simulating the conditions, time of day and track features you may find on test day.

☐ **Local Location**

If the facility is local, go there and practice or walk the site. Become familiar with the surroundings, building placements, potential scent traps, dead end corridors. Talk with other exhibitors who have trained or attended test at this site. Try to determine how the tracks were planned, where the dogs had problems and work on practicing on these potential problems.

☐ **Travel Location**

Arrive a few days early and walk the site, plotting tracks as if you were the judges. Verify with the test committee that it will be permissible for you to be on site. Do not go anywhere near the site on the day the judges will be plotting the tracks.

☐ **Judges**

Research the judges for the test. Are they working their dogs on variable surface, teaching VST classes or perhaps they already have a VST title on their dog? Do you consider them to be your equal in VST tracklaying ability? Do you feel they can understanding when your dog is activity searching or simply wandering? Do they have a reputation for quick whistles, poorly designed tracks and excuses for why they had to blow off a dog that may have been checking a scent pool? Do they understand scent and how it travels and pools around variable surfaces? Do you feel that the judges are qualified to judge your dog? These are the questions you must ask before you enter a test.

Unless you are willing to invest your time with the understanding that the test will be an expensive training track, do not enter a test with unqualified judges hoping that you, your dog and the judges will all have a *good day* and you will pass. Sadly, most likely it will not happen.

Chapter 31

About the Authors

Ed Presnall

A software developer and consultant to the computer industry, Ed and his wife Peggy, have been involved in the breeding and training of English Springer Spaniels and Clumber Spaniels for over twenty years.

The recipient of numerous titles in conformation, obedience and tracking, Mr. Presnall spends a majority of his time now as a tracking instructor and published author. A supporting member of the Dog Writers Association of America, his articles and stories are seen in numerous published dog-related magazines, newsletters and web sites on the World Wide Web.

Pictured above with his English Springer Spaniel "*JJ*", Ch. Kay N Dee Hiddenbrook Rampage CD, TD, VST, the first VST Spaniel of any breed, the 6th dog and the first TD dog to earn the VST *and* his Clumber Spaniel "*Merlin*", Ch. Andchelle Lord Raglan TD, VST the first Clumber Spaniel and the 9th dog to receive the title.

Christy Bergeon

A regional marketing manager for a major computer component manufacturer, Christy and her husband Steve have been involved in training German Shepherd Dogs and Schipperkes for over ten years.

Pictured here above "*Ariel*", Jendhi Shepherd's Jigger, TD, VST, the 8th and youngest dog to receive the VST title.

Together, Ed and Christy teach basic and variable surface tracking classes, offer seminars and workshops on Variable Surface Tracking and continue to work on VST with their dogs.

Why Do We Track?

We started tracking for the simple reason that it was fun and enjoyable to spend time in the field with our dogs.

Many trackers take younger dogs, which are growing up and are not involved in conformation, field or obedience to allow these dogs to mature while experiencing unpressured training. This seems to help many of the young dogs "get their head straight" before formalized competition. Tracking is also the next logical step for that dog which has its Championship. As one of our friends like to state, "*The best dogs are those with a title at each end.*"

Another reason is to allow the older or retired dog to remain active while working in a non-competitive and hopefully stress-free arena. But the vast majority of trackers do it just because they love to be outside, exercising while spending time with a dog and their friends.

With the introduction of VST, tracking to us has become an obsession. The integration of variable surfaces into our basic TD tracking program has allowed us to strive for better results with our young dogs. Developing new and easier training methods such as **Component Training** has allowed our dogs and our students to accelerate the training process and become *test ready* in months and not years.

Most of all it has given us a method, through our training, that we can give something back to the sport. We are proud to be a supporter of VST and will continue to strive to help educate and promote the sport.

PHOTO BY CHRIS PRESNALL

Chapter 32

Our Dogs and Their VST Tracks

V S T

Making Tracks

Articles by Ed Presnall

JJ's Story - The Dog Nobody Wanted ...
Ch. Kay N Dee Hiddenbrook Rampage CD, TD, VST
VST Number 6, June 22, 1997
The First VST Spaniel and The First TD Dog To Earn a VST

Ariel's Story - The Team
Jendhi Shepherds' Jigger TD, VST
VST Number 8, October 5, 1997
The Youngest Dog To Earn a VST

Merlin's Story - Twice As Nice
Ch. Andchelle Lord Raglan TD, VST
VST Number 9, October 5, 1997
The First VST Clumber Spaniel

The Dog Nobody Wanted ...

by Ed Presnall

"JJ" was the pick of the litter, a very nice show puppy. He was one of the few survivors of a catastrophic motor home fire, had been shuffled through multiple combinations of owners and finally returned to his breeder who died shortly thereafter. From there, his journey continued. In his last home, due to the owner's work schedule, it was mandatory that he be crated for long periods of time. This did not sit well with either "JJ" or his owner. The owner quickly decided that, once again, "JJ" needed a new home.

The trauma from the fire, multiple homes and owners had built up insecurity, claustrophobia and separation anxiety in this wonderful dog.

We opened our hearts and our home to him almost four years ago as his eighth home in four years. When he arrived at the airport in Houston, even heavily sedated, he had partially destroyed his kennel in an attempt to escape. Such was my introduction to this "special" dog. For many months, he could not be left alone or crated. He escaped from every run and enclosure and always seemed concerned that he would be dumped wherever we went. Even today, he cannot be crated out of our sight.

I started taking JJ for rides in the van to watch as I trained one of my other dogs in tracking. After a few weeks, he would bark every time the other dogs came to a corner or found the glove. After five weeks of his watching and our listening to him bark at the tracking exercise, we tested him on a simple track and he showed that he was both a quick learner and a natural tracker. His desire to please, combined with his competitive nature was overcoming some of his anxiety problems.

He quickly mastered the basics of tracking and on a cold day in December, JJ along with one of our Clumbers, received his TD, in back-to-back tracks, after only four and a half months of training.

He was sporadically entered in conformation where he frequently won the breed and had garnered a few group placements in a very tough Sporting Group. His performances in conformation were anything but lackluster, however, it was obvious that he and I were both addicted to tracking. In an effort to assist him in his recovery, we removed him from conformation competition to allow him to continue with tracking. He went to all of my classes and became a "demo" dog for corners and turns.

We had worked on TDX for almost a year when one day he became ill. The vet diagnosed him with several large tumors in his throat and mouth. We discussed our options and brought in a surgical specialist to remove tumors. JJ went through the operation without much hope of success.

His determination took over as he slowly recovered. The vets were adamant that he not be worked for at least six weeks following surgery. JJ would whine when I took the other dogs out tracking. Once again I started taking him along again "to watch" and soon he convinced me that he wanted to try again. Last fall we entered the ESS Tracking Dog Excellent test in Detroit and after a very long drive, we did not pass. We began working diligently on variable surface and he started to really progress.

Now, we can say that Variable Surface Tracking (VST) has come of age for the Spaniel community. A new type of tracking, VST became an official AKC event in 1995. The sport is considered by many trackers and the AKC as the future of tracking. With the continued reduction of available space to hold tracking events, this new test involves the use of urban areas such as colleges, industrial parks, business areas and other typical non-tracking sites.

Unlike the normal Tracking Dog (TD) or Tracking Dog Excellent (TDX) tests, a VST track is plotted on, as the name implies, variable surfaces. The track must include three different surfaces, which shall include vegetation and at least two areas devoid of vegetation. Non-vegetated areas can include concrete, asphalt, gravel, sand, hard-pan or mulch.

As we trained down here in the tropics of Houston with high heat and even higher humidity, I looked forward to some cool weather and an opportunity to work with JJ somewhere other than in a steam bath.

We made the long drive from Houston to Chicago for the Glenbard All Breed Obedience Club, Inc. VST test on Sunday, June 22. When we arrived, it was hotter in Chicago than it had been in Houston. So much for planning.

The site for the test was a County Government complex in Wheaton, IL. As we arrived, I thought it was actually a college campus, divided by a large, "not lightly traveled" road. About eight buildings and a small lake on one side of the road and seven buildings and two large ponds on the other side. The entire site is about 150 acres of tracking heaven.

Large expanses of manicured grass and multiple blacktop parking lots, divided by islands filled with mulch, wood chips and some plants faced the entrants. Stone, gravel, dirt and concrete were also available for the various surfaces. Just for fun, the planners of this complex threw in a few hundred geese and ducks to entice the sporting dogs which might venture to this lovely site. It is a beautiful location suitable for five long tracks, and is to me, an example of what "urban tracking" is all about. Hopefully more clubs will find similar locations to expand this sport.

We drew track three which was located near the headquarters building. The first two tracks were across the road, so while a Welsh Corgi Pembroke and a Doberman ran their tracks, we sat in the heat, baking like chicken on a grill, and waited for the judges to return. By the time it was our turn, the sweat was pouring off of me and JJ was very hot and had lost most of his motivation. As we walked to the start, he looked up at me as if to say, "but you promised me cool weather".

We approached the start, I put on his harness and led him to the start flag which was located three feet from a sidewalk. He downed at the flag and we went through our routine of allowing him to settle in and sniff the article, while I took several deep breaths. When we were ready, he strongly indicated the track direction for about ten feet. Then, he proceeded to put on the worst display of a start I have ever seen. He came back and sat at my feet. Re-scented ... he started again and came back and laid down ... it was the longest three minutes of my life and for a moment I really though it was just too hot for him to work.

Since we have been working large asphalt expanses, his grass work has become somewhat questionable, but I trust him. When he gives me a direction, I believe him, so even though he had only gone ten feet, I felt he was right. I knelt down and told him that we had come a long way and even if it was hot, we needed to get going. I looked down and told him that he knew where the start was, he had told me the direction and if he wanted to track down the sidewalk instead of on the grass it was OK with me.

He put his nose down and tracked confidently down the sidewalk while I followed like the "dope at the end of the rope". He checked the grass twice during the first 24 yards, then crossed a blacktop road and progressed up the sidewalk in front of the county jail building. It was visiting hours and a mother and child were walking across a parking lot towards us. At about 110 yards, JJ indicated a turn into the parking lot and looked left to see people were coming out of the jail building and right to be faced with the woman and child. The woman confidently told her child that it was "OK to pet the nice doggie". I held my breath and prayed for him to remember his show ring training. He walked into a perfect stack, wagged his tail and acted like a proper show dog, while the child hugged and petted him. Finally they walked on and I took another breath.

I knelt down again to help give him motivation and a small drink of water, and re-scented him. He looked left again and then started off right into the parking lot. We crossed 18 yards of blacktop and went up on a 6 yard island filled with mulch. He shifted right a few yards and continued on across another 22 yards of blacktop to another island. This was a wide mulch filled island with a large sidewalk about 15 feet wide down the middle of it. He sharply turned left and headed down the sidewalk for 130 yards. The farther we went on the non-vegetated surfaces, the stronger he pulled and the more determined he became. At the end of the sidewalk, we crossed a blacktop street to the grass in front of the courthouse building. He checked right, around an evergreen tree, and then went left behind a bus stop shelter and up a wheelchair ramp to the front doors of the courthouse.

He was confident across 27 yards of brickwork and down the other wheelchair ramp. Suddenly he turned right into a flower bed and started crittering. We had a very brief discussion about this not being the time for him to play with a lizard and he shot left for 20 yards across the grass near a chain link fence to a white object on the ground. As I approached the potential article, I saw that it was the plastic lid to a coffee cup.

When I reached down to pick up the coffee cup lid, a door opened about fifteen feet away and a line of ten or twelve prisoners in orange jump suits, each shackled together, exited the building to our left. The prisoners moved along the fence, talking among themselves about JJ and stood near a waiting van. Ignoring the new distraction, JJ restarted and went about 20 yards down the fence line to a stone path under a large portico. He threw on the brakes and started indicating that an article or turn was nearby. He looked left, then right around a large post and found a leather wallet in the gravel. We had now gone 380 yards.

We continued across the grass into a tunnel of blacktop, grass and chain link fencing. Fences right and left with a blacktop road down the middle. He indicated the track was on the right side in the grass, near the curb. He was confident as he strode 75 yards down the blacktop to a open turn onto an adjoining street. To our right was a large hill with a railroad track at the top. On our left was the wide blacktop road we had just crossed and beyond it, high fencing for the jail area.

JJ stepped out of the street and onto the grass next to the curb and headed down the shoulder. About 75 yards later he indicated a metal article. We had now gone 563 yards. Off we went again for 75 yards of grass and an open left turn into the street. Twenty yards of blacktop and 18 yards of grass later JJ entered a parking garage.

As I entered the dark garage from the bright sunlight, he was standing near a pile of trash. A small rope, a coffee cup and some paper. He checked each as a potential article and near the curb he located a small plastic coffee can lid with the number 4 drawn on the top. As I grabbed the article, JJ jumped into my arms.

I lifted the article above my head and clutched JJ to my chest, only then did I hear the crowd for the first time. We had gone 703 yards, officially 387 on vegetation and 316 non-vegetated, but JJ had worked about 400 yards of non-vegetated surfaces. I removed his harness and we strode into the sunlight to shake the judges' hands and have everyone pat JJ for his achievement. The dog nobody wanted, had succeeded in doing what many said could not be done.

He will now be known as Ch. Kay N Dee Hiddenbrook Rampage CD, TD, VST, an English Springer Spaniel. Only the sixth dog to earn this title, the first Spaniel of any breed and the first dog to pass this test without the advanced TDX title.

Now, JJ and I will continue to work on tracking and animal assisted therapy and he will occasionally be shown in the conformation ring to show that this Springer, "the dog nobody wanted", really can do it all!

PHOTO BY CHRISTY BERGEON

**Ed Presnall and "JJ" with Judges
Darlene Ceretto and Mel Lloyd**

PHOTO BY CHRISTY BERGEON

**Ed Presnall and "JJ" with
John Barnard**

The Team

(c) 1997, Ed Presnall

As I watched, my first thought was that if this was in black and white and not real life, I'd be watching a slapstick Charlie Chaplin movie.

Across the field was a young lady with a very nice looking puppy. While the puppy danced and pranced in circles around her, she was comically trying to both untangle the lead and buckle on the harness, in preparation for their first lesson. The harness was only halfway on, the lead wrapped around both the handler and dog, and as I watched I simply had to smile.

I'd seen it before. Soon the handler would give up and start yelling either at the dog or hopefully for assistance. I watched carefully. Something about this young lady and this dog was different. She quickly removed the harness, untangled the lead and calmly started over. After two or three attempts, she completed the task.

Like most people who get involved in tracking learn, repetition is the key to being successful. Even something as simple as putting on a harness will take a time or two to get the proper procedure down pat. I walked across the field to introduce myself.

The handler's name was Christy and her GSD was named Ariel. Soon I learned that Ariel was from a well known breeder with great success in the show ring as well as in the field. I also learned that Christy, having been involved with Schipperkes for years, had selected this breed and this dog to fulfill her desires for a working dog. She talked of having an "all round" dog which could compete in herding, agility obedience and tracking. I'd heard that story before to, from too many first day students.

As we spent the next few weeks working on basic training. Out of the corner of my eye, I always watched Christy and Ariel work their lesson plan. My admiration for them grew. They were, as I had first thought, different. They worked together as a team from the first day, gaining confidence from each other.

As the classes continued, I found myself working more and more with Christy and Ariel. We laid a few extra tracks and worked on some of the tougher scenting problems which she might face in her TD test. The dog required challenges to excel while Christy asked endless streams of questions which often made me rethink my training methods.

As test day neared, I knew that this team was ready. She certified easily and made the draw for the fall test. We worked harder and longer on the difficult scenting problems, changes in the length of grasses, small ditches and a multitude of things which they might encounter in the test. During the weeks before the test, we haunted the test site, a county park only a few minutes away, laying tracks, which had been used in previous tests by other judges, to prepare them for their test day.

When the big day came, they drew track number one and passed in style. Christy had been watching me train my Springer in variable surface tracking and shortly after the test asked if we could work together.

Due to an illness with one of my dogs, it was several months later before we actually started working together on VST. As we progressed, we implemented more and more unusual and unorthodox training procedures into our practice and Christy and I became a team working together to reach our goals. Together we devised methods to motivate the dogs and keep their interest as we tracked over miles of asphalt, concrete, mulch and dirt.

Three months later we entered a test. I passed with my Springer and watched with pride as Ariel worked the first half of the track magnificently before being distracted in a large parking lot. The long drive home was a frustrating time for me. I had passed and was very happy, but Christy had failed. We promised each other that we would work even harder and try again.

We tracked at night using flashlights in areas where there were no street lights. Learning to blindly follow our dogs in and around the scent cone which moved and swirled around buildings. Heaping praise on our dogs when they were right and motivating them when they faced seemingly insurmountable problems. Each night we learned a little more and each time we went out we came up with new questions and problems to challenge both us and the dogs.

We planned tracking around our real jobs during the week and around our home life on weekends. At times, I'm sure, our families thought we had run off to be tracking gypsies, but we trained on through the heat, rain and dark of night. When we felt we were ready, we entered another test.

On the night that Christy was notified that she had made the draw and would run, I was told I would be an alternate and therefore most likely not participate. We decided to make the long drive together as a team so that I could be there to offer support. A few days before we left, I received a message that one of the entrants had withdrawn to attend another test and I would be allowed to run. The team was again heading north, to prove that variable surface tracking was an attainable goal.

As we waited on the judges for the start of her track, we talked of all the preparations we had made. We instilled confidence in each other and promised that we would do our best and let our young dogs do the work of proving they were ready.

As she walked across the street with her harness in her hand and Ariel by her side, I was proud. She had come a long way from being a student to being my partner in a training program. In seven short months, we had taken two young TD dogs and turned them into confident trackers on variable surfaces.

The start was on short grass for 47 yards with a right turn about 10 yards before a drop off to a loading dock to a building. Ariel made the first corner sharply and continued on for 60 yards where she turned left between two buildings for an additional 68 yards of grass before entering an asphalt parking lot. Five yards later, Ariel indicated the second article (fabric). The track continued on asphalt for 28 yards where it turned right for one of her moments of truth. Not missing a beat, Ariel executed the turn and proceeded another 75 yards on asphalt to a curb and sidewalk in front of a small metal building and a communication tower.

The tower was surrounded by approximately 30 feet by 30 feet of high chain link fencing. As Ariel approached the sidewalk and chain link fencing, she appeared to be drawn down the fence and away from the track. After about 30 yards and checking out the back doorway of this building and 3 unclaimed newspapers, she recovered and returned to the track and proceeded down the side of the metal building on a concrete driveway.

After 25 yards on cement, they crossed 5 yards of mulch, 15 yards of blacktop driveway and proceeded another 25 yards, stepped over a curb and proceeded 8 yards across grass. Facing them was a very high traffic road. The track turned left on grass for 15 yards, crossed a blacktop driveway and proceeded another 25 yards on grass to a left turn between a building and parking lot entrance to a Nursing Home. After another 25 yards on grass, Ariel indicated the third article (metal). The track continued down the grass island for 55 yards to an open turn to the right across 6 yards of grass and out into the parking lot.

Ariel worked diligently determining the proper place to step into the parking lot. Faced with a long row of cars, she searched intently up and down the row and finally decided to enter the parking lot next to a Mercedes, one car off from the track. The area was heavily contaminated from both automobile and pedestrian traffic in the parking area. As she came out into the main portion of the parking lot between the cars, Christy and Ariel were confronted by an elderly resident of the nursing home in an wheelchair. The chair was parked directly on the last turn and when she spotted Christy and Ariel, proceeded toward them directly on the next to last leg of the track in the parking lot. While the woman rolled down the track she said *"Honey, I'm not afraid of dogs, bring your dog over here for me to pet it"*. The woman continued to advance on the team.

Although the judges tried to wave the woman in the wheelchair off the track, she was oblivious to what they wanted and merely waved back. At that point, the woman in the wheelchair was pushing Christy and Ariel off the track as she kept rolling towards them. The judges told Christy to "hold up" and one of the judges approach the woman in an attempt to draw her off the track as she appeared to be confused. After a brief and humorous discussion with the lady, who wanted to be pushed around the parking lot, she and her oxygen tank were deposited near the nursing center door to the cheers and grins of the spectators.

After Christy re-scented Ariel, they continued to work this portion of the track. She executed a nice open left turn on asphalt, went 60 yards on asphalt, crossed a grass island about 10 yards wide and across another 50 yards of asphalt. As she moved through the parking lot, she headed left of a Stop Sign in a barrel which was located in the center of the parking lot. When she reached the Stop Sign, she gave an excellent indication of an article and started a circular search. Ariel located the final article, a plastic lid, about 10 yards to the right of the Stop Sign.

A tear rolled down my face as I watched my partner and her dog locate the final article on their track and triumphantly hold it up for the world to see, thus becoming Jendhi Shepherds' Jigger TD, VST, the youngest dog to ever attain the Variable Surface Tracker title!

As I ran across the parking lot to congratulate them, I thought back to that first day and to all the goals we had reached since then. I was right, they were different. They worked as part of a team breaking down problems, setting goals and reaching upward for that golden ring. They we part of my team, and I was proud of them.

PHOTO BY ED PRESNALL

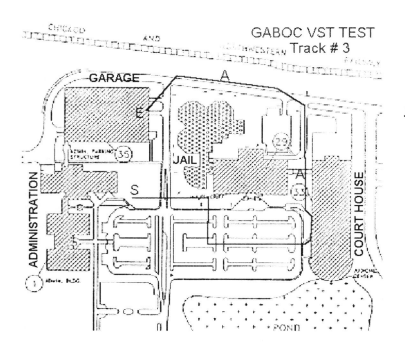

GABOC VST TEST
Track # 3

VST # 6

Glenbard All Breed Obedience Club
DuPage County Government Center
Wheaton, Illinois
June 22, 1997
Judges: Darlene Ceretto & Mel Lloyd
Track # 3

**Ch. Kay N Dee Hiddenbrook
Rampage CD, TD, VST
Call Name - "JJ"**
English Springer Spaniel (d)
Age: 8 years 1 month old
Handler: Ed Presnall

Yardage: 703, NV 387, 316 V
Track Age: 3 hours and 15 minutes
Start Time: 9:25am
Run Time: 20 minutes
Weather: Sunny/Hot
91 degrees/73% humidity
Wind: Nil

VST # 8

Glenbard All Breed Obedience Club
DuPage County Government Center
Wheaton, Illinois
October 5, 1997
Judges: Darlene Ceretto & Wally O'Brien
Track # 1

**Jendhi Shepherds' Jigger TD, VST
Call Name - "Ariel"**
German Shepherd Dog (b)
Age - 2 years 5 months
Handler - Christy Bergeon

Yardage: 656, 304 NV, 352 V
Start Time: 9:50am
Run Time: 30 minutes
Weather: Sunny/Warm
75 degrees/50% humidity
Wind: Nil

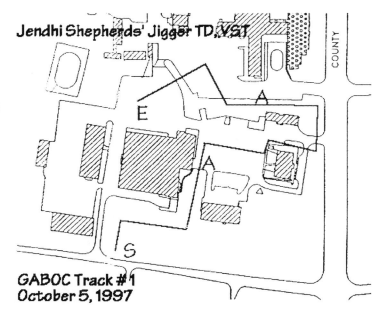

GABOC Track #1
October 5, 1997

Twice As Nice

(c) 1997, Ed Presnall

The walk from the van to the start flag in a tracking test is a long one. There is, sometimes, perhaps too much time to relive earlier tracks and errors you might have made. To second guess your training or the ability of your dog at a time like this is a mistake too many make during the trek to the flag.

For me it is a time to think back about my dog and all of the things we have done together. We are prepared, we know that as a team we are unbeatable, we are positive! As we walked I thought back over the past few months and the accomplishments of the "*never give up*" attitude this dog and this breed has.

I remembered that it was only ten months ago to the day that our vet had said that Merlin was going to die and he did not know why. The vets were stumped. As the process of total shutdown of his kidneys progressed, we watched him fade, but always with the strength to wag his tail or give us one more sloppy lick.

I remember asking for assistance with my friends on the Internet and getting a recommendation from a vet and fellow Clumber owner over 1,400 miles away. My vet discarded the recommendation as a waste of time and money to run such specialized tests. I recalled my determination as I refused to accept his opinion or heed his warnings and carried Merlin to the van. In a last minute effort to save him, I raced through the night, fighting a rare ice storm, to the vet school over a hundred miles away.

But most of all, I remembered that Merlin never gave up. My friend on the Internet was correct, the specialists at the university quickly diagnosed Merlin as having contracted two very rare strains of Canine Leptospirosis. Serovars were pomona and tarassovi. Pomona had only been diagnosed in one case in the US in the previous 15 years and tarassovi, in canines it was thought, had rarely been seen outside of Russia. But with treatment and the ever present Clumber stamina he recovered and continued his training.

I thought back to our 1,200 mile drive to this place and the hours of discussion with my tracking partner. Our determination to work in this new sport and to learn as much as possible with our willing dogs. The hundreds of questions we asked and the use of sometimes unorthodox training methods. We cussed and discussed the months of practice tracks in the sauna we call Houston. Heat indexes during much of the summer exceeded 100 degrees as we laid the tracks, and sometimes dipped down into the 90's as we ran them. Smiling, I recalled the tracks late at night, carefully planned to time our running with the automatic sprinkler systems. A reward for our hard work and an opportunity to let both the handlers and the dogs cool off.

The thousands of yards of track we laid each week had paid off in a very short time frame. The dogs were steady and sure of the track and had become confident and somewhat exhilarated by the numerous challenges and scent obstacles we'd put them through. During this period, we had learned that the dogs could track on asphalt, concrete and rocks almost as easily as they crossed the manicured lawns surrounding the buildings of our training sites.

Grinning to myself, I remembered my pride only a few moments earlier as I watched my partner and her dog locate the final article on their track and triumphantly hold it up for the world to see, thus becoming the youngest dog to ever attain this coveted title.

Now Merlin, my Clumber Spaniel, and I stood at the start of our Variable Surface Tracking (VST) track, attempting to do what no Clumber had done before. Our friends and supporters were in the crowd watching as the judges nodded that they were ready. As I snapped on his harness and laid out the long line, I quietly reassured Merlin and myself that we could do it!

The start was in a large grass field. Merlin had a good start and proceeded 105 yards, made a nice right turn for 25 yards and crossed a large berm surrounding a big parking lot. Without missing a step, he crossed 50 yards of asphalt and made a perfect 90 degree turn to the left (one of his moments of truth). After the hard surface turn he crossed another 20 yards of asphalt, a mulch island and 20 more yards of asphalt. Exiting the parking lot onto grass he again crossed a large berm and entered a grass field for another 60 yards.

He turned right and continued for 35 yards where he stopped and stood, indicating an article. As I approached him, I did not see an article. He was very excited, with his tail wagging and looked up at me as if to say, "Well, it was here". He restarted and continued on. Merlin is a very intense tracker, and a good problem solving dog. He simply refused to admit that the article was missing. He started a precise and somewhat frustrated search in a grid pattern, looking for the "lost" article. On four separate occasions, he returned to the last corner and finally convinced himself that the article was not going to be found.

Merlin returned to the track and proceeded 25 yards, executed a 90 degree right turn on grass towards a building. After 20 yards, he entered a covered alcove and proceeded 25 yards on stones to the brick wall of the building. Appearing still to not be satisfied that he had not found the "lost" article, he backtracked across the stones to the grass, re-executed his last turn and attempted to return to the spot where he had indicated the article. During this trek, we encountered the Judges, who were rushing to catch up after we had turned the corner of the building. Merlin stopped in front of the Judges and I explained, with a grin, that he was still not satisfied.

Seemingly, the confrontation of the Judges had given him a solution to his puzzle of where the missing article might have gone. He looked in the direction of the spectators and quickly returned to his track and retraced his steps to the building. Once again crossing the 25 yards of stone, he turned left at the brick wall and followed the edge of the building across stone, grass, and a cement pad to the end of the building. He continued on across a grass area and a sidewalk where he stepped out into another asphalt parking lot.

He proceeded onto the asphalt for 13 yards and made a very sharp 90 degree turn to the right, continued through the parking lot for 70 yards where he downed at a leather wallet. Restarting, he worked 15 more yards of asphalt heading towards a mulch island. In the asphalt, before the island, he executed an open turn to the right. The track followed the end of a line of four islands across the parking lot for 72 yards. Stepping off of the asphalt onto a grass island, he immediately downed to indicate his final article, a plastic reflector.

As I raised the article over my head, he jumped into my lap. I held him for a moment before Merlin, the first VST Clumber, turned his attention to the gathering crowd.

I had returned to Illinois for this test, to a site very similar to our training area in Houston, with a goal in mind. Ironically, Merlin and I stood only a few yards from where his companion and house mate JJ became the first VST English Springer Spaniel three and a half months earlier. Once again we had done what many said could not be done.

As I shook the judges' hands and Merlin received praise from the crowd, I watched as my tracking partner quietly approached. We congratulated each other and silently walked together back towards the van. With smiles of satisfaction on our faces and two good dogs at our side, we knew that it was, like they say, *"Twice As Nice"*!

**Ed Presnall and "Merlin" and
Christy Bergeon and "Ariel"
With Judges Darlene Ceretto and Wally O'Brien**

**(l-r) Wally O'Brien, Christy Bergeon, Ed Presnall
Jean Greenwalt and Darlene Ceretto**

Searching for the lost article ...

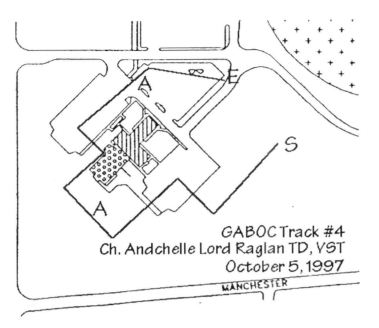

GABOC Track #4
Ch. Andchelle Lord Raglan TD, VST
October 5, 1997

MANCHESTER

VST # 9

Glenbard All Breed Obedience Club
DuPage County Government Center
Wheaton, Illinois
October, 1997
Judges: Darlene Ceretto & Wally O'Brien
Track # 4

Ch. Andchelle Lord Raglan TD, VST
Call Name - "Merlin"
Clumber Spaniel (d)
Age: 4 years 7 month old
Handler: Ed Presnall

Yardage: 602, NV 287, 315 V
Track Age: 3 hours and 10 minutes
Start Time: 10:52am
Run Time: 32 minutes
Weather: Sunny/Hot
75 degrees/50% humidity
Wind: Nil

Component Index